JOURNEY OF MY

I0517733

A PATH TO SELF DISCOVERY & EMPOWERMENT

JAMIE L. O'NEILL

ISBN: 978-1-968061-14-2

Dedication

To Todd, thank you for always believing in me and seeing my light even when I struggled to find it myself. Your unwavering love has been a constant, and for that, I am forever grateful.

To my children, you are my heart, my greatest purpose, and the reason I continue to grow.

To everyone who has been part of my journey, whether through love, lessons, or both, thank you for shaping my story in ways I never expected but always needed.

And to Frank, thank you for being my mirror, for challenging me, and for reminding me what it truly means to love without limits.

Table of Contents

Your Invitation to the Greatest Adventure of Your Life

Alright, consider this your official invite to one of the wildest, most rewarding journeys you will ever take. The journey inward. No packing required, no passport necessary, and definitely no hiking boots, unless you are really committed to the aesthetic. This is an exploration of the deepest parts of yourself, where the only baggage you need to unpack is the emotional kind. And yes, there might be a few tears, but think of them as soul-level detox rather than a tragic meltdown over a stubbed toe. This book is your trusty companion, a slightly snarky but endlessly supportive guide to navigating self-discovery. If my guided journal, *Journey of My Soul*, is the map, then this book is the enthusiastic tour guide here to help you go deeper, laugh harder, and embrace the magic of who you really are. In a world full of distractions, it is easy to lose yourself in the chaos. One minute, you are scrolling social media, and the next, you are questioning your entire existence while trying to figure out why every single sock you own has mysteriously disappeared. Between the noise, the expectations, and the endless to-do lists, it is no wonder so many of us feel disconnected from our true selves. But here is the good news. Everything you are searching for is already inside you. Your intuition, your purpose, your peace, and your potential are all hanging out, waiting for you to tune in. This book will help you tap into that inner wisdom, uncover what has been buried beneath the stress and self-doubt, and start living in alignment with who you were always meant to be. The *Journey of My Soul* journal was designed to guide you back to yourself with thought-provoking prompts and a little bit of tough love wrapped in inspiration. This book takes it further. It is packed with insights, stories, and just enough sarcasm to keep things interesting. And because I believe in full transparency, I will be sharing my own journey. The messy parts. The hard parts. The holy-shit-how-did-I-survive-that parts. Addiction. Awakening. Transformation. It is all in here. My story is proof that no matter where you are starting from, change is possible. And not just possible, but more fulfilling than you might expect. Together, we will dive into the art of self-discovery, the power of authenticity, and the strength that comes from resilience. We will explore what it means to align with your soul's purpose, navigate life's inevitable plot twists, and manifest a life that reflects the person you truly are. This book is for anyone who is ready to reconnect with themselves. Whether you are just beginning this journey or have been on the path for years, my hope is that these pages will become a source of clarity, inspiration, and maybe even the occasional kick in the ass to remind you of the power you hold. So, as you turn each page, keep your heart open and your mind curious. And for the love of all things holy, do not forget your sense of humor. This is your journey. It will be messy, beautiful, unexpected, and completely yours. Now, let's get started.

Your Invitation to a Life-Changing Habit

If you have never journaled before, consider this your official invitation to start. No RSVP required, just a willingness to put pen to paper and see where it takes you. If you are already a seasoned journal junkie, let this be your reminder to keep going, to keep digging, and to keep showing up for yourself in ways you never imagined possible. Journaling is not just about venting your frustrations or cataloging your day. Some days definitely deserve a full-page rant, but it is also about peeling back the layers and uncovering the truths that have been buried under years of conditioning. It gives you the space to explore who you really are without the noise of outside opinions clouding your judgment. Every time you write, you create a space where your thoughts, emotions, and desires can be seen, acknowledged, and understood. You are not just reflecting on where you have been. You are actively shaping where you are going. This practice has the power to shift your perspective, reveal hidden patterns, and spark the kind of clarity that leads to real, meaningful transformation. So here is my challenge to you. Pick up a journal, crack open that blank page, and just start. No pressure, no perfection required. Just a raw, honest conversation with yourself. Let your words flow without censorship, without second-guessing, and without worrying if you sound deep enough. This is not about writing something profound. It is about writing something true. This book is not just a guide. It is an invitation. A reminder that every word you put on the page is a step toward something greater. A deeper connection. A clearer path. A more authentic you. Grab your favorite notebook, trust the process, and start writing your next chapter. One that is truer, freer, and unapologetically yours.

Chapter 1

Exploring the Soul—A Journey Through Spiritual and Philosophical Perspectives

"The journey of the soul is a sacred unfolding, where every step, whether in light or shadow, guides us closer to the truth of who we are meant to be." —Jamie

The Soul. Yeah, That's a Big One.

Just saying the word feels heavy, doesn't it? Like it is carrying centuries of mystery, a sprinkle of existential dread, and enough unanswered questions to make your head spin. What is it? Where does it come from? Does it live forever, or does it just peace out when our bodies call it quits? People have been asking these same questions since the beginning of time, and guess what? Nobody has a definitive answer. But one thing is crystal clear. The soul is the core of who we are. It is the part of us that exists beyond skin, bones, and that weird knee pain that shows up out of nowhere. It is the eternal spark that makes us unique, the quiet inner voice that usually knows what's up before our brains can catch on, and the reason some of us just cannot shake the feeling that we are meant for something more.

I have felt that pull my whole life. When I was a little kid, I would lie in bed at night, staring at the ceiling, trying to figure out why I was here. Not just in the "what am I supposed to be when I grow up" kind of way, but the deep, soul-level "why do I even exist" kind of way. I knew there had to be something bigger than just waking up, eating cereal, going to school, and repeating the cycle. Life had to be more than just existing in a body. There was something inside me that felt vast, something that made me feel connected to something beyond myself, something I could not quite put into words. That feeling never went away. If anything, it grew stronger over time, pushing me toward the work I do today.

Since ancient times, humans have been obsessed with figuring out this whole soul thing. Different cultures, religions, and philosophies have all taken their best shot at explaining it. Some see the soul as a divine gift, a sacred piece of something much greater than ourselves. Others believe it is an infinite traveler, hopping from lifetime to lifetime, collecting wisdom like a spiritual hoarder. Even science, which loves a good "prove it or lose it" moment, has been stumped by the concept of consciousness and what makes us, well, *us*.

So, what exactly is the soul? Is it energy? Is it spirit? Is it just a collection of memories and emotions getting passed around like an old, well-loved book? Truthfully, no one can answer that for you. Your soul is yours to define, yours to experience, and yours to explore. But what we *can* do is dig into some of the different ways humanity has tried to understand it, laugh at the absurdity of it all, and maybe even uncover a little more about ourselves in the process.

Because at the end of the day, whether the soul is a divine spark, a cosmic hitchhiker, or just a beautifully unexplainable part of existence, one thing is for sure. You are more than just a body walking around trying to find the meaning of life. And if you have ever had that deep, gut-level knowing that you are here for something bigger, congratulations. You are officially on the right track.

A VIP Pass to Your Inner World

Think of your soul as the ultimate VIP of your existence. It is the backstage pass to your deepest truth, the part of you that existed before this life and will continue long after. It is your guide, your teacher, and, at times, your biggest challenger. It nudges you toward growth, whispers wisdom in the quiet moments, and occasionally smacks you upside the head when you refuse to listen (not literally, but you get the point). The soul is what connects you to something greater, whether you call it God, Source, the Universe, or simply a feeling of oneness. It is what reminds you that you are here for a reason, even if that reason sometimes feels as clear as mud. And trust me, that is part of the journey.

The Soul According to the World's Religions and Philosophies

Religions and philosophies have been trying to crack the code on the soul for centuries, each with their own version of what it is, where it goes, and why it matters. Some believe the soul is an eternal, divine spark, while others think it is a temporary visitor that pops in, learns a few lessons, and then moves on. No matter the interpretation, one thing is clear. The soul is kind of a big deal. It is the thing that makes you, well... *you*, the unseen force that carries your experiences, your dreams, and your moral compass.

Now, if the idea of a cosmic courtroom, a reincarnation cycle, or a grand universal reunion makes your head spin, do not worry. We are about to break it all down in a way that is entertaining, digestible, and maybe even a little irreverent.

Christianity: The VIP Pass to Eternity

In Christianity, the soul is basically your golden ticket to the afterlife. Handcrafted by God and built to last for eternity, it is the core of your identity, the divine breath that makes you more than just a walking bag of bones.

The Christian playbook says that once your earthly gig is up, your soul stands trial in the ultimate celestial courtroom. God is the judge, and depending on how you lived—whether you were a saint, a troublemaker, or somewhere in between—your next stop is decided. Heaven is the ultimate paradise, Hell is the less-than-ideal alternative, and Purgatory is the waiting room for those who need a little extra soul scrubbing before heading up to the pearly gates.

So, according to Christianity, your soul is not just a placeholder for your personality. It is the essence of who you are, tied to your choices and carrying your moral resume straight into eternity. No pressure.

Hinduism: The Ultimate Spiritual Recycling Program

In Hinduism, the soul, or *Atman*, is not just a part of you. It *is* you. Your real, unchangeable, eternal self. Your physical body? Temporary. Your overthinking brain? Also, temporary. The *Atman*, however, is the spark of divinity within you, and it is on a journey far bigger than this one lifetime.

But the *Atman* does not just get a free ride. It is stuck in *samsara*, the endless cycle of birth, death, and rebirth, collecting karma points along the way. Good deeds push you toward a better next life, while bad ones... well, let's just say you might find yourself coming back as something less glamorous than you were hoping for.

The grand prize in Hinduism is *moksha*, liberation from this never-ending loop. Once you reach it, your soul merges back with *Brahman*, the ultimate reality. Think of it as logging out of the game of life for good and finally becoming one with the universe.

Buddhism: The No-Soul Soul Theory

Buddhism throws a bit of a curveball when it comes to the soul. Unlike other traditions that see the soul as something permanent and unchanging, Buddhism says, "Nah, that is an illusion." Enter *Anatta*, the idea of "no-self."

Instead of a single, eternal soul hanging around, Buddhism teaches that we are more like a flowing stream of consciousness, constantly changing. The energy that makes us who we are gets carried forward through karma, but there is no permanent "you" tagging along from one life to the next.

And what is the goal? Reaching *Nirvana*. This is the ultimate mic-drop moment where you break free from the cycle of suffering and stop the karmic wheel from spinning. It is not about making the soul better. It is about realizing that the soul was never really a fixed thing to begin with.

Islam: The Eternal Soul on a Divine Path

In Islam, the soul, or *ruh*, is straight from God, breathed into the body at the time of creation. It is your built-in connection to the divine, kind of like spiritual Wi-Fi, always on and always connected.

The soul is immortal, which means when your physical body taps out, the soul keeps going. But here is the catch. On Judgment Day, your soul reunites with your body to face the ultimate evaluation. The verdict determines whether you are heading to eternal paradise or to a place that is, well, *less* pleasant.

Your soul starts off pure, but life has a way of tossing temptations and distractions at it. The good news? Redemption is always on the table, and no matter how much dust your soul has gathered, you can always give it a good polish through faith, prayer, and righteous living.

Ancient Greek Philosophy: The Ultimate Throwdown

The Greeks were absolutely obsessed with the soul. They debated it, wrote about it, and probably got into a few drunken shouting matches over it. Two of the biggest names in the game, Plato and Aristotle, had wildly different takes, and honestly, if they were alive today, their Twitter fights would be legendary.

Plato was all in on the idea that the soul was immortal, floating around in the universe before we were even born, just waiting to drop into a body like some cosmic Uber ride. He saw the body as nothing more than a temporary prison, trapping the soul until it could finally break free and head off to the afterlife. To make things even more complicated, he divided the soul into three parts. First, the rational side, the one that actually thinks things through. Then, the spirited side, which is all about ambition, courage, and probably yelling at referees during a game. And finally, the appetitive side, the one that just wants to binge-watch reality TV, eat an entire pizza, and take a three-hour nap. According to Plato, if you let the rational part take the wheel, you were on the path to wisdom. If you let the appetitive side run the show, well, good luck with that.

Aristotle, on the other hand, was not here for any of that "floating, immortal soul" nonsense. He thought the soul was what gave a body life and purpose, but the second you kicked the bucket, that soul was out of business. No body, no soul. End of discussion. Where Plato saw the soul as an eternal, independent entity just waiting to escape its human meat suit, Aristotle saw it as the battery that powered the body. No more power, no more function.

So, who was right? That is the fun part. We still do not know. But what we do know is that this ancient Greek debate is still going strong, which means these guys really did leave their mark. Whether you are team Plato or team Aristotle, one thing is clear. The Greeks may be long gone, but their ideas are still stirring up arguments, and let's be honest, that is kind of impressive.

Descartes: The Mind-Body Tag Team

Fast-forward a couple of millennia, and we meet René Descartes, the guy who gave us "I think, therefore I am." He introduced *dualism*, the idea that the mind (or soul) and the body are two completely separate things. The body handles the physical world, while the soul takes care of thoughts, emotions, and self-awareness.

Descartes even suggested that the soul and body meet up for top-secret business in the pineal gland, a tiny part of the brain he thought was the hub for all mind-body interactions. Modern neuroscience might not agree with him, but his theory set the stage for centuries of debates about consciousness and the nature of the soul.

Existentialism: Make Your Own Meaning

Then came the existentialists, the philosophers who basically said, "Forget pre-written destinies. You create who you are." Jean-Paul Sartre argued that there is no predetermined soul or essence. Who you become is based on the choices you make. Life is a blank canvas, and you are the one holding the brush.

Nietzsche went even further, tossing out traditional ideas of the soul altogether. He saw life as a process of constant evolution, with each person responsible for shaping their own identity. No divine plan. No cosmic roadmap. Just raw potential waiting to be realized.

Daoism: Balance is Everything

Daoism takes a more fluid approach, seeing the soul as a balance between two forces. *Hun* is the spiritual, airy side that floats toward the divine, while *Po* is the grounded, physical part tied to the body. They need to stay balanced for a harmonious life.

When life ends, *Hun* and *Po* return to the *Dao*, the ultimate flow of the universe. Instead of a judgment day or a reincarnation cycle, Daoism sees death as a return to the cosmic rhythm, a peaceful merging with the infinite.

Mystical and Esoteric Interpretations

Step aside, mainstream religion and philosophy. The mystical and esoteric traditions have arrived, bringing their own brand of deep, mysterious, and sometimes downright mind-bending takes on the soul. These belief systems do not just accept the soul as some passive, prepackaged part of existence. Oh no, in these circles, the soul is a work in progress, a constantly evolving masterpiece that requires dedication, self-discovery, and a willingness to dive headfirst into the unknown.

Here, spiritual growth is not just encouraged. It is the entire point. The soul is not something you simply *have*. It is something you are meant to refine, transform, and elevate. Think of it as the ultimate personal development project, but instead of just trying to be a better person, you are working toward something even bigger. The grand finale? A full-blown union with the divine, where you merge with the cosmic source in a way that defies human comprehension.

These traditions take the journey of the soul to a whole new level, one where mystical experience, hidden knowledge, and sacred teachings guide the way. Whether you are decoding ancient symbols, diving into past-life memories, or exploring the vast depths of your own consciousness, the esoteric path is anything but boring. It is an adventure filled with secrets, revelations, and the kind of soul expansion that makes the whole journey worth the effort.

Kabbalah: The Mystical Onion of the Soul

In Jewish mysticism, specifically Kabbalah, the soul is kind of like an onion. Not because it makes you cry, although spiritual enlightenment *can* be an emotional rollercoaster, but because it has layers. Lots of them. Peel one back, and there is always another waiting underneath, each revealing a deeper, more profound truth about who you are and why you are here.

According to Kabbalah, your soul is made up of three main layers. *Nefesh*, which is the animal soul, *Ruach*, which is the spirit, and *Neshamah*, which is the divine soul. Think of these like levels in a spiritual video game. You start off with the basics, just trying to survive, but as you level up, you gain wisdom, insight, and a stronger connection to the universe. Instead of collecting coins or magical weapons, you are gathering soul points, unlocking higher awareness, and hopefully avoiding unnecessary respawns.

Level One: Nefesh — The Survival Mode

Nefesh is your starter pack, the soul's ground floor. It is the part of you that handles all the basics. Eating, sleeping, running from danger, and making sure you do not walk into traffic while scrolling your phone. This is the primal, instinct-driven aspect of your being, the part that keeps you tethered to the material world. It is not bad, just basic. Like the tutorial level of a game, it teaches you how to function before you move on to anything more advanced.

At this stage, your soul is focused on existence itself, handling the everyday needs that keep you alive. It is like that first stage in *The Legend of Zelda* where you are just running around with a wooden sword, trying not to get wrecked by low-level enemies. Necessary? Absolutely. But the real adventure is still ahead.

Level Two: Ruach — The Emotional Expansion Pack

Once you have mastered the basics of survival, it is time to move up to *Ruach*, the emotional and moral layer of the soul. This is where things start getting interesting. If *Nefesh* is all about staying alive, *Ruach* is about figuring out why you are alive in the first place.

Here is where you develop your sense of self, form deeper connections with others, and start having actual opinions about life. Morality, emotions, and personal growth all live here. It is like moving from basic button-mashing to a game that requires strategy and skill. You are no longer just reacting. You are making conscious choices, figuring out what matters to you, and trying to play the game in a way that aligns with your values.

Ruach is where relationships come into play, both with people and with the divine. You start asking big questions, feeling things more deeply, and realizing that life is not just about surviving but about finding meaning.

Level Three: Neshamah — The Cosmic Cheat Code

And then there is *Neshamah*, the ultimate upgrade, the final boss level of the soul's journey. This is the highest, most refined layer, where your soul is no longer just existing or searching for meaning. It is reaching for divine connection. *Neshamah* is where you stop seeing life as a puzzle to solve and start recognizing that you are part of something so much bigger than yourself.

At this stage, you are not just playing the game. You are seeing the code behind the game itself. You understand the patterns, the lessons, and the deeper purpose behind everything. You are no longer just seeking God. You are experiencing God in a way that transcends logic, religion, and human understanding.

This is the level where mystics, sages, and deeply spiritual seekers operate. They are not just dabbling in enlightenment. They are living it. And while most of us are still trying to get out of *Ruach* without getting stuck in an existential crisis, *Neshamah* is waiting for the ones willing to keep climbing.

Reaching Neshamah isn't about perfection or having all the answers— it's about surrender. It's a quiet knowing that even in your most uncertain moments, you are held by something infinite. You stop needing to control the journey and start trusting the unfolding. And the irony? The higher you go, the more grounded you become—because true spiritual wisdom doesn't float above life. It *roots* you in it with reverence, humility, and awe.

The Kabbalistic Quest for Divine Connection

The Kabbalistic journey is about moving through these soul levels, peeling back the layers, and working toward spiritual enlightenment. Through meditation, study, and a whole lot of self-reflection, you start clearing away the clutter of everyday existence and tuning it into the bigger picture. This is not a quick journey. It is a lifelong process of growth, self-discovery, and breaking free from whatever is keeping you stuck in the lower levels.

Kabbalah does not see the soul as a fixed, unchanging thing. It is always growing, shifting, and evolving. It is a work in progress, a never-ending adventure of trying to get closer to the divine while still dealing with all the everyday nonsense of being human. The deeper you go, the more you uncover about yourself, the universe, and the spiritual forces at play.

So, if you ever feel like you are just scratching the surface of your spiritual potential, you probably are. There are always more layers to uncover, more insights to gain, and more levels to reach. Whether you are in survival mode, deep in self-discovery, or ready to unlock the highest truths, the path is waiting. Just keep peeling back those layers.

Sufism: The Soul's Ultimate Ego Detox

Sufism, the mystical side of Islam, sees the soul as a divine spark on a mission to get back home to God. Think of it as the ultimate road trip, except instead of packing snacks and a killer playlist, you are shedding all the useless baggage you have been dragging around for lifetimes. No overpriced gas station pit stops, just a deep, spiritual purge of everything that is holding you back from true enlightenment.

This journey is not for the faint of heart. Sufism is all about stripping away the layers of ego, attachment, and general human nonsense that cloud your soul. It is like spring cleaning but for your entire existence. All those petty desires, fears, and illusions that keep you tied to material distractions? Time to toss them in the metaphorical trash. Sufis believe that these things act as a thick, murky veil between you and God, blocking you from experiencing divine truth. The goal is to clear away all that junk until your soul is pure enough to reflect the divine light like a freshly polished mirror.

Fana: When Your Ego Bites the Dust

The final destination on this trip is *Fana*, which is the total annihilation of the self. And no, that does not mean poof, you disappear. It means your ego gets booted out of the driver's seat so that you can fully merge with the divine. Imagine a single drop of water falling into the ocean. That drop does not cease to exist, it just becomes one with something infinitely larger. This is not about losing yourself in some dark abyss, it is about dissolving all the false layers of identity that keep you separate from God.

Sufis do not stop at *Fana*, though. That would be too easy. Once you have obliterated your ego and achieved oneness with the divine, you move into *Baqa*, where you exist within God's presence while still maintaining a sense of self. Think of it like reaching enlightenment but still being able to function in the world without floating off into the void. It is spiritual transcendence with a side of practicality.

Dancing Your Way to Enlightenment

If all of this sounds a bit heavy, just know that Sufis have found a pretty poetic way to embody this soul journey. Ever seen those whirling dervishes spinning around in a trance-like state?

(I had a great time watching them while visiting Egypt) That is not just for show. It is a physical meditation, a dance of devotion that represents the soul's movement toward unity with the divine. The longer they spin, the deeper they fall into a state of pure connection, until there is no dancer, only the dance. No self, only the presence of God.

Sufism is not about saving your soul. It is about purifying it, refining it, and stripping away every illusion until what remains is nothing but divine love. It is a path of deep devotion, endless self-reflection, and an unwavering commitment to letting go of the things that keep you small. The ultimate goal? To burn away everything false and become a living embodiment of divine truth. No ego, no bullshit, just pure, unfiltered connection with God.

The Soul's Modern Makeover: A Remix of Ancient Wisdom

Fast forward to today, and the idea of the soul has gotten a bit of a facelift. It is less about ancient doctrine and more about blending old wisdom with modern curiosity. Imagine it as a spiritual remix, where the timeless beats of sacred teachings meet the fresh rhythms of psychology, philosophy, and science.

Gone are the days when the soul was strictly defined by religious dogma. Now, we have a buffet of perspectives to choose from. Some people still vibe with the classic spiritual traditions that see the soul as eternal, others lean into psychology, where the soul is more of a reflection of consciousness, identity, and emotion. And then there is the wild world of quantum physics, where scientists are throwing around theories about energy, consciousness, and dimensions that sound eerily similar to what mystics have been saying for centuries.

At this point, the soul has become a mash-up of different ideas, all pointing toward the same thing. Understanding who the hell we really are. Whether you are into Eastern spirituality, ancient philosophy, or cutting-edge neuroscience, the modern soul is like a kaleidoscope. Every turn shifts the perspective, revealing another layer of what makes us human.

Spirituality today is less about rigid belief systems and more about finding what resonates. Think of it like curating a personal playlist for your soul. Take a little wisdom from the Buddhists, a bit of Sufi poetry, throw in some Jungian psychology, and maybe sprinkle in some scientific musings on consciousness. The result? A unique, ever-evolving understanding of the soul that actually fits your journey.

At the end of the day, the modern soul is about exploration. It is about staying curious, questioning everything, and carving out your own path toward self-discovery. Whether you see the soul as a spark of the divine, a shifting part of your psyche, or a connection to some vast cosmic force, one thing is clear. The journey to understanding it is one hell of an adventure.

Carl Jung and the Soul: Your Psyche's Director

Carl Jung was not here for surface-level psychology. He dove straight into the depths of the unconscious mind and found that the soul is not just a quiet observer. It is the main character in the story of your psyche, shaping your thoughts, behaviors, and experiences behind the scenes.

Jung saw the soul as a bridge between the conscious and unconscious, linking our personal experiences with something much bigger. Enter the *collective unconscious*, the universal memory bank of symbols, archetypes, and ancient wisdom that connects every human being across time and space. Think of it as the spiritual internet, where every soul is plugged into a vast database of shared human experience.

Jung's concept of *individuation* is basically the soul's personal development plan. The goal is to integrate all parts of yourself, including the stuff you shove into your psychological junk drawer. That shadow self you would rather ignore? Time to bring it into the light. The wounds and insecurities you keep avoiding? They are waiting to be acknowledged. The more you embrace every part of yourself, the closer you get to wholeness.

According to Jung, the soul is not some mystical concept floating around in space. It is woven into everything we do, every dream we have, every moment of deep self-reflection. Whether you call it the higher self, the unconscious mind, or something entirely different, the soul is always there, nudging you toward growth, whether you like it or not.

New Age Spirituality: The Soul's Cosmic Choose-Your-Own-Adventure

In the New Age world, the soul is less about rigid definitions and more about personal exploration. It is seen as an eternal consciousness, bouncing through lifetimes, learning, evolving, and gathering wisdom along the way. Instead of a one-and-done deal, life is a never-ending series of incarnations, each one a new chapter in the soul's epic journey.

Here, reincarnation is not just a theory. It is a full-blown cosmic curriculum. Every life is a lesson, every challenge is a test, and every connection is part of a much bigger picture. Some believe that before we are born, we choose our experiences, relationships, and hardships to help our souls grow. Basically, we sign up for this mess willingly, which is either deeply profound or completely insane, depending on how your life is going.

The New Age take on the soul is all about interconnectedness. The idea that every soul is part of a massive, ever-expanding universe, constantly learning, shifting, and evolving toward something greater. Whether that is enlightenment, divine union, or just becoming a more self-aware human, the journey never really ends.

At its core, the soul's modern evolution is about freedom. The freedom to explore, to question, to redefine what spirituality means on your own terms. No more rigid boxes, no more one-size-fits-all beliefs. Just a never-ending quest for truth, meaning, and the realization that maybe, just maybe, we are all part of something bigger than ourselves.

Dolores Cannon's Wildest Past Life Cases: Buckle Up for a Cosmic Roller coaster

Dolores Cannon was not just a hypnotist. She was a metaphysical detective, a fearless explorer of the weird, the mystical, and the downright mind-blowing. I am a huge fan of her work and her teachings. Using her *Quantum Healing Hypnosis Technique* (QHHT), she guided clients into deep trance states where they tapped into past life memories, interdimensional experiences, and some seriously trippy cosmic downloads. Some stories were so detailed, so bizarre, and so historically accurate that they left even the biggest skeptics scratching their heads.

If you think past life regression is just about remembering a quiet medieval farm life or a tragic Victorian romance, think again. Dolores' clients recalled everything from being extraterrestrial beings to working with high-tech energy crystals in Atlantis. So, sit back, grab a drink, and prepare to have your mind blown as we dive into some of the wildest cases she ever documented.

The World War II Fighter Pilot Who Remembered Going Down in Flames

One client found themselves reliving life as a fighter pilot during World War II, and let's just say this was not some vague dreamlike vision. The details were **insane**. They described the inside of the aircraft down to the buttons and levers, the sheer rush of flying, and the split-second horror of being shot down. The moment of death hit them like a punch to the gut. The emotions, the fear, and even the sensation of impact were so real that their body reacted as if they were actually dying all over again.

Here's the kicker. After the session, some digging revealed that the pilot they described had actually existed, and the circumstances of his death matched the details perfectly. This was not some general war memory pulled from a history book. This was real, firsthand, terrifyingly accurate.

Atlantis: The Lost City of Advanced Crystal Tech

Atlantis might be the most overused ancient mystery of all time, but according to multiple clients, it was not just a myth. Dolores had more than a few sessions where people recalled living in Atlantis, and they were not just lounging around in togas. One client described working with advanced crystal technology that was light-years ahead of anything we have today. These massive crystals were used for energy, healing, and some next-level science that would make modern physicists cry.

But, of course, humanity being humanity, they got a little *too* ambitious. The misuse of this power and the gradual drift away from spiritual principles led to the downfall of this once-thriving civilization. Greed and ego won out, and Atlantis went full *Titanic*, sinking both literally and metaphorically. If these accounts are to be believed, humanity had its shot at utopia and, well, totally botched it.

The Time a Client Was an Alien (Yes, Really)

Not all past lives happened on Earth. Dolores Cannon had plenty of clients who skipped the whole human experience entirely and recalled lifetimes as extraterrestrial beings. One client described life as a non-human entity on another planet, complete with specific physical features, an entirely different environment, and a civilization that was light-years ahead of Earth's mess.

This particular being belonged to a peaceful, advanced society that was sent on missions to observe and assist with Earth's evolution. Think *cosmic babysitters*, but with a much higher IQ. Many other clients reported similar experiences, with Dolores collecting an entire library of alien past lives, proving that the soul's journey is not limited to this little rock we call home.

Ancient Egypt's Healer Extraordinaire

One client went way back, recalling a life as a healer in ancient Egypt. Not the snake-oil, wave-your-hands-over-the-wound kind, but a true spiritual and medicinal practitioner. She described working inside a temple, using herbs, sacred incantations, and energy healing to cure the sick. She rattled off details of rituals and spiritual beliefs that were later found to match known Egyptian healing practices.

Even wilder, her current life's obsession with holistic healing suddenly made sense. Turns out, she had been at this whole *healer thing* for more than just one lifetime. Her past life was simply picking up where it left off, showing that the soul's work does not stop just because the body does.

Lemuria: The Forgotten Civilization of Nature and Energy

Atlantis gets all the press, but Lemuria? That is a whole other story. Another client remembered living in this lost civilization, which supposedly predated Atlantis and was deeply connected to the Earth's energy. These people were highly intuitive, had a telepathic connection with each other, and knew how to work with natural forces in ways that would make today's scientists weep.

Lemurians lived in perfect balance with the planet, using the Earth's energy for healing and communication. But much like Atlantis, things eventually went south. A shift in consciousness, natural disasters, and possibly some good old-fashioned human arrogance led to the fall of yet another ancient civilization. If these past-life stories are accurate, history has been repeating itself for *a very long time*.

The Spanish Inquisition Nightmare

Not all past lives were filled with wisdom and wonder. Some were brutal. One client found themselves right in the middle of the Spanish Inquisition, and let's just say it did not end well. They recalled being accused of heresy, tortured, and ultimately executed.

The emotions and physical sensations were so intense that the client's body reacted as if they were being tortured all over again. This past life explained their deep-rooted fears of authority, persecution, and even seemingly irrational anxieties they had never understood before. Sometimes, your baggage is not from childhood trauma. It is from getting burned at the stake a few hundred years ago.

The Native American Connection

One client remembered a life as a Native American, long before European settlers arrived. They described the tribe's deep spiritual connection with nature, their traditions, and their way of life in perfect detail. The experience was so vivid that it left the client in tears, reconnecting them to a sense of identity they had never fully understood.

This past-life regression helped them heal deep feelings of displacement and loss in their current life, as if their soul was mourning something it had experienced long ago. It was a reminder that the echoes of past lives can still shape who we are today.

Alien Abductions: Past and Present

Dolores Cannon also had a fair share of clients who recounted being abducted by extraterrestrials. Some had memories from their current lives, others recalled encounters from past lifetimes. One client described being taken aboard a spacecraft, subjected to various procedures, and later realizing that these experiences were not random. They were part of a bigger plan.

According to Dolores, these encounters were often tied to the soul's mission and had a purpose within a larger cosmic framework. Whether you believe it or not, these stories suggest that some souls are playing an entirely different game than the rest of us.

The Soul's Journey is One Hell of a Ride

Dolores Cannon's work peeled back the layers of reality, revealing that the soul's journey is **anything but boring**. Her clients uncovered past lives in ancient civilizations, lifetimes as extraterrestrials, and encounters with otherworldly beings that make sci-fi movies look tame.

Whether these experiences were literal or symbolic, one thing is clear. The soul does not just stick to one lifetime, one body, or even one planet. It is on a wild, multi-dimensional adventure, collecting wisdom, evolving, and sometimes crashing and burning along the way.

So, if you have ever felt like you do not quite belong here, maybe you have been here before. Or maybe, just maybe, you are one of those cosmic travelers passing through Earth for a brief, chaotic visit. Either way, Dolores Cannon's work suggests that the story of the soul is far bigger, far weirder, and far more incredible than we ever imagined.

Why Self-Discovery is the Ultimate Life Hack

Getting to know yourself is like unlocking a cheat code for life, except instead of unlimited money or instant success, you get something even better. Clarity. Confidence. A life that actually makes sense. Self-awareness is the foundation of everything. It is the difference between stumbling around in the dark and flipping on the light to see exactly where you are going. When you truly understand yourself, everything starts to click. Relationships become healthier, choices become clearer, and you stop wasting time on things that drain your energy.

Think of self-discovery as your internal GPS. When you know what drives you, what lights you up, and what absolutely does not, you can navigate life without constantly second-guessing yourself. You stop living on autopilot and start making choices that actually align with who you are. It is like tuning into your own personal radio station where every decision plays a song that just feels right.

This is not about becoming some perfectly enlightened all-knowing guru. It is about peeling back the layers of conditioning, expectations, and societal nonsense that have piled on over the years and getting to the raw, unfiltered truth of who you really are. When you stop living for external validation and start honoring your inner voice, you shift from just existing to actually thriving.

A self-aware life is not just about feeling good. It is about living with intention. It is about making choices that serve you instead of ones that keep you stuck. It is about embracing your strengths, accepting your flaws, and realizing that every part of you, even the messy, complicated, weird parts, deserves to be seen and celebrated.

At the end of the day, self-discovery is not just important. It is essential. It is the difference between a life that feels forced and one that feels yours. So do the deep dives, ask yourself the hard questions, and embrace the journey. Because the more you uncover about yourself, the more you realize that the person you have been searching for has been there all along just waiting for you to finally see them.

Alignment with Core Values: Living in Sync with Who You Really Are

Understanding yourself starts with getting crystal clear on your core values. These are not just feel-good words you slap on a vision board. They are the deeply ingrained principles that shape how you make decisions, handle relationships, and move through the world. When you truly know what matters to you, life stops feeling like a chaotic free-for-all and starts making a whole lot more sense.

Living in alignment with your values is like finally stepping into the right rhythm. Everything just flows better. If honesty is one of your core values, choosing truth in every aspect of your life will bring a sense of ease and fulfillment. It is like your soul giving you a standing ovation for staying true to what actually matters. You feel whole. You feel grounded. You feel like you are living a life that actually fits.

But when you start betraying your values, things get messy fast. Ignoring what you truly believe in leads to an internal battle that no number of distractions can drown out. That nagging feeling of unease? That is your soul throwing up red flags, trying to snap you out of it. Maybe you convince yourself to stay in a job that crushes your spirit or maintain relationships that drain the life out of you. Trust me here, I am the QUEEN of staying in relationships way past the expiration date! At first, it might seem manageable. But over time, that disconnect will chew away at your happiness, leaving you restless, unfulfilled, and wondering why everything feels just a little off.

And let's be real. The deeper you stray from your values, the louder that inner voice gets. It will not whisper. It will scream. It will keep you up at night, remind you in quiet moments, and show up as frustration, anxiety, or even full-blown existential dread. That is the price of living out of alignment, and no amount of forcing it will make the discomfort disappear.

The truth is alignment with your core values is not just some self-help buzzword. It is the difference between a life that feels like a constant struggle and one that feels like it is actually yours. So, get clear on what matters. Set boundaries that protect those values. And for the love of all things holy, stop settling for situations that go against the very core of who you are. Because once you start honoring your truth, everything else has a way of falling into place.

Purpose and Direction: Get Your Shit Together and Own It

Self-awareness is like having an all-access pass to your own damn life. When you actually know what excites you, what you are naturally good at, and what makes you want to throat-punch boredom, you stop wasting time on things that do not matter. Instead, you start moving with purpose. Every choice, every action, every step you take suddenly has meaning because it is aligned with what *you* want, not what someone else thinks you *should* want.

Without self-awareness, though, life becomes one giant game of "What the hell am I even doing?" You float from one thing to another, filling your days with activities that look great on paper but leave you feeling as empty as a bag of chips after a stress-eating session. Sure, you are busy, but are you actually fulfilled? Probably not. If you have ever found yourself knee-deep in a situation wondering, *Why am I even here?*, congratulations. That is what happens when you move through life without purpose.

Getting to know yourself is not just about navel-gazing and self-reflection. It is about making sure your life actually feels good instead of just looking good from the outside. When you have a solid grasp on what makes you come alive, you start building a life that is not just tolerable but actually fulfilling.

Improved Relationships: Stop Settling for Half-Assed Connections

One of the best perks of deep self-awareness? You start attracting the right people while cutting ties with the energy vampires and emotional leeches who drain the life out of you. When you understand your needs, boundaries, and emotional triggers, you stop wasting time in relationships that feel forced, one-sided, or straight-up exhausting. The list of people I have had to boot out of my energy field is enough to create a whole basketball team!

Knowing yourself means you communicate better. You are not fumbling around trying to please everyone or swallowing your feelings to keep the peace. You can say what you need, mean what you say, and build relationships that do not require you to shrink yourself to make others comfortable. That is the difference between real connections and surface-level nonsense.

And let's talk about compatibility. When you are tuned into who you are, you naturally start surrounding yourself with people who actually *get* you. No more forcing friendships out of convenience or staying in relationships out of habit. Instead, you find your people. The ones who see you, respect you, and celebrate you without conditions. When you stop pretending to be something you are not, you give the right people the chance to actually *find* you. I have been so blessed to find a community of beautiful souls at my spiritual sanctuary... The Kava Bar! I will talk more about that later.

Emotional Resilience: Learn to Take Life's Punches Without Falling Apart

Understanding yourself is not just about knowing what makes you tick. It is about knowing how to keep your shit together when life decides to throw a curveball straight at your face. Emotional resilience is what separates the people who crumble at the first sign of trouble from the ones who take a hit, wipe the dust off, and keep going.

When you are self-aware, you stop reacting like a human time bomb every time something goes wrong. Instead of spiraling into panic mode, you pause, assess, and actually *deal* with what is happening. You become your own emotional detective, figuring out why you are feeling what you are feeling and handling it like the badass you are.

Life will always have its ups and downs. That is just the deal. But when you have emotional resilience, you do not just *survive* the chaos—you learn from it, grow from it, and come out stronger than before. The real flex is not avoiding challenges. It is knowing you can handle whatever the hell comes your way.

Empowerment and Confidence: Give Less Fucks, Live More Freely

The second you stop seeking outside validation and start trusting yourself, life gets a whole lot better. When you truly know who you are, you stop giving a damn about whether other people approve of your choices. Instead, you make decisions based on *your* truth, not on what society, your family, or that random person on social media thinks you should be doing.

This kind of confidence is not about pretending you are perfect. It is about owning your strengths, acknowledging your flaws, and realizing that none of it makes you any less worthy. You are not here to fit into some pre-approved mold. You are here to live unapologetically, to stand firm in your beliefs, and to trust that you are capable of making decisions that serve *you*.

The more you embrace this mindset, the less you find yourself looking for outside approval. You stop waiting for permission, stop explaining yourself, and stop second-guessing every little move. You just *do*. And that kind of confidence? It is magnetic. It is the kind of energy that attracts the right opportunities, the right people, and the kind of life that actually feels like your own.

Authentic Self-Expression: Stop Playing a Role and Just Be You

Self-awareness is the ultimate key to finally showing up as your real self in every part of your life. No more playing roles. No more watering yourself down to fit someone else's expectations. No more feeling like you must ask for permission to be exactly who you are.

Authentic self-expression is about aligning with the truth of who you are and letting that shine in everything you do. It means embracing your weirdness, your quirks, and the things that make you different instead of trying to hide them. It means putting your energy into things that actually light you up instead of doing what is expected just to keep up appearances.

And when you start living this way, something amazing happens. You attract people, opportunities, and experiences that actually resonate with *you*. No more chasing things that do not fit. No more forcing yourself into spaces where you do not belong. The more you own your truth, the more your life starts to reflect it back to you.

At the end of the day, knowing yourself is not just about personal growth. It is about freedom. The freedom to live life on your own terms, to walk away from anything that does not serve you, and to finally stop playing small. The world does not need a watered-down version of you. It needs you exactly as you are. So, own it!

Personal Growth and Transformation: The Never-Ending Glow-Up

Self-understanding is the foundation of personal growth. When you actually know what you are good at, where you need some work, and what patterns keep tripping you up, you stop running in circles and start making real progress. This is where you take the reins, face your fears head-on, and break the cycles that have kept you stuck. Growth is not about becoming some polished, perfect version of yourself. It is about leveling up, one hard-earned lesson at a time.

Self-discovery is not a one-and-done process. It is a lifelong adventure where each breakthrough brings you closer to the best, most authentic version of you. You are constantly evolving, upgrading, and rewriting the script on who you are and what you are capable of. The more you grow, the more you realize that the journey itself is where the magic happens.

Inner Peace and Contentment: The Real Flex

Knowing yourself on a deep level is the key to real, unshakable inner peace. When you are in tune with who you are, you stop feeling like you are playing a role in someone else's script. You stop chasing approval, forcing yourself into situations that drain you, or pretending to be someone you are not. Instead, you create a life that actually *fits*, one that makes sense for *you*.

That alignment between who you are on the inside and how you live on the outside? That is the good stuff. That is the kind of peace that no amount of money, status, or outside validation can ever replace. It is the feeling of knowing you are exactly where you are meant to be, doing exactly what you are meant to do, without second-guessing every damn thing.

And the best part? The more you honor your truth, the easier it gets. No more forcing yourself into situations that feel wrong. No more wondering if you are living the way you are *supposed* to. You just *are*. And that is freedom.

Beginning the Journey: Time to Dive In

Understanding yourself is not a final destination. It is a lifelong journey filled with self-reflection, messy realizations, and some much-needed reality checks. It takes curiosity, patience, and a willingness to dig deep. Ready to start? Here is how you can kick things off.

1. Pay Attention to Yourself: Self-Awareness is the First Step

The first step in getting to know yourself is actually paying attention. Sounds simple, right? But most people go through life on autopilot, reacting to things without stopping to question *why*. Self-awareness means becoming an observer of your own thoughts, emotions, and actions.

Start by asking yourself:

- What emotions came up for me today? What triggered them?
- How did I react in different situations, and why?
- What thoughts have been running through my mind, and how do they shape my actions?

Journaling is a game-changer here. Writing things down helps you see patterns, connect dots, and uncover truths you might otherwise ignore. Over time, you will start recognizing habits, thought cycles, and emotional triggers that reveal *exactly* what is going on under the surface.

2. Get Curious and Drop the Judgment

Self-discovery is not about labeling yourself or stuffing yourself into a neat little box. It is about peeling back the layers and seeing what is underneath. And to do that, you need to get *curious*.

Ask yourself *why* you think the way you do? Why you react a certain way? Why you avoid certain things or crave others? Get real with yourself but ditch the self-judgment. This is not about beating yourself up for past mistakes. It is about getting honest and seeing yourself clearly, flaws and all.

When you start exploring yourself with curiosity instead of criticism, you open the door to real change. You stop trying to be who you think you *should* be and start embracing who you *actually* are.

3. Figure Out Your Core Values

Your core values are not just words that sound nice. They are the principles that shape your life, whether you realize it or not. When you are clear on them, decision-making becomes a hell of a lot easier. You stop wasting time on things that do not align with what truly matters to you.

To figure out your core values, ask yourself:

- When in my life have I felt the most fulfilled? What values were being honored?
- When have I felt deeply uncomfortable or conflicted? What values might have been ignored or compromised?
- What beliefs do I refuse to sacrifice, no matter what?

Once you have your answers, take a hard look at your life. Are you actually living by these values, or are they just words you like the *idea* of? If you are out of alignment, it is time to start making some shifts.

4. Set Intentions for Your Growth

Self-discovery is not about creating rigid goals that box you in. It is about setting clear intentions that guide you in the right direction. These are not rules, they are reminders of what you are working toward.

Ask yourself:

- What do I want to get out of this journey?
- How do I want to feel as I explore and uncover more about myself?
- What qualities do I want to cultivate in myself?

Write them down, revisit them often, and adjust them as you grow. Your path will shift, and that is okay. The key is to keep checking in with yourself and making sure you are still headed where you *want* to go.

5. Practice Mindfulness and Actually Pay Attention

Mindfulness is not just about meditating or sitting in silence. It is about being present in your own damn life. It means noticing your thoughts instead of letting them run the show. It means tuning into your emotions instead of pushing them down. It means actually experiencing your life instead of constantly thinking about the past or stressing about the future.

Ways to practice mindfulness:

- Breathe. Take deep, intentional breaths when you feel overwhelmed.
- Be present. Whether you are eating, walking, or having a conversation, give it your full attention.
- Observe. Notice your thoughts and feelings without immediately reacting to them. Let them come, acknowledge them, and decide what to do with them.

The more you practice, the more self-aware you become. And that awareness is what leads to real, lasting change.

6. Get Comfortable with Being Uncomfortable

Self-discovery is not all rainbows and feel-good moments. It requires vulnerability. It means facing the parts of yourself you would rather ignore. The fears, the insecurities, the old wounds you have buried. Growth lives in that discomfort. If you want real change, you have to be willing to sit with the hard stuff.

Vulnerability is not a weakness. It is a superpower. It is what allows you to build deeper connections with yourself and others. It is what helps you break through the barriers holding you back. So, lean into it.

7. Try New Things and Expand Your Comfort Zone

You do not find yourself by doing the same thing over and over again. You have to push your limits, challenge yourself, and experience things you never have before.

- Try new hobbies or activities.
- Travel to places that force you to see the world differently.
- Engage in conversations that challenge your perspective.

Every new experience adds another layer to your understanding of yourself. Growth does not happen in the comfort zone. It happens when you step out and see what you are truly capable of.

8. Be Patient and Let the Journey Unfold

Self-discovery is not a straight path. It is a winding, unpredictable, sometimes frustrating adventure. There will be moments of clarity that feel like breakthroughs and moments of confusion that make you question everything. Both are valuable.

You will make mistakes. You will change your mind. You will evolve in ways you never expected. That is the whole point. Give yourself permission to be a work in progress.

The more you embrace the process, the more fulfilling it becomes. This journey is yours. Make it count.

Chapter 2

Embracing Authenticity – Owning Who You Are Without Apology

"Embracing authenticity means daring to show the world who you truly are, without apology, knowing that your uniqueness is your greatest strength."
—Jamie

As you dig deeper into your journey of self-discovery, one of the most powerful realizations you will come across is the absolute necessity of living authentically. Now, let's get one thing straight. Authenticity is not just some feel-good buzzword slapped onto motivational posters. It is the real deal. It is about stripping away the layers of conditioning, expectations, and societal nonsense to reveal who you truly are at your core. And in a world that loves to tell you who you should be, choosing to be your unapologetic self is not just bold. It is revolutionary.

What Does It Actually Mean to Be Authentic?

Being authentic is not about playing a role or trying to fit into a box that someone else built for you. It is about living in alignment with your deepest truths. Your values, beliefs, passions, and desires. It is about speaking your mind, honoring your emotions, and showing up in life as the unfiltered, real version of yourself. Think of it as finally stepping into clothes that fit just right instead of squeezing into something that makes you feel like a stranger in your own skin.

Being authentic means embracing every part of yourself, including the messy, complicated, and imperfect bits. It is about knowing who you are and owning it with confidence instead of watering yourself down to be more acceptable to others. When you live authentically, you stop performing and start living. You no longer feel the need to shape-shift depending on who is watching because you are finally comfortable in your own damn skin.

But let's be honest. Society does not exactly roll out the red carpet for those who refuse to conform. From childhood, we are taught to color inside the lines, follow the rules, and mold ourselves into something that fits the world's expectations. And while structure can be useful, it can also be suffocating when it pressures us to betray who we really are for the sake of belonging.

The Battle Between Authenticity and Conformity

I spent years wrestling with the need to be accepted. Like many people, I grew up hyper-aware of how others perceived me. Their opinions shaped my actions, my choices, and even my sense of self. I became a master of people-pleasing, constantly second-guessing myself to ensure I fit into whatever mold was expected of me at the time.

For me, this struggle was deeply tied to the traumas I experienced in my early years. When you grow up in survival mode, authenticity is not always an option. It felt safer to be who others wanted me to be rather than risk rejection by being myself. I learned to silence parts of me that felt too loud, too much, or simply inconvenient. Over time, I lost sight of where the real me ended and the version of me built for others began.

I became addicted to validation. I craved the approval of others because, deep down, I had no idea how to approve of myself. Every decision I made was filtered through the question, *Will this make me more likable? More acceptable? More worthy?* It was exhausting, and worse than that, it was a losing game. Because no matter how hard I tried, I could never win over everyone. And in the process of trying, I abandoned the one person whose approval truly mattered—my own.

Reclaiming My Authentic Self

Breaking free from this cycle did not happen overnight. Learning to embrace my authentic self has been a long, messy, and sometimes uncomfortable journey. But with every step I take, I feel lighter, more whole, and more at peace with who I am.

For me, authenticity means reclaiming the parts of myself I once hid. It means speaking my truth without worrying if it is too much. It means showing up as I am, even when I know not everyone will like it. It means embracing my past, my struggles, my quirks, and my strengths as integral pieces of who I am instead of things to be fixed or hidden away.

The biggest lesson I have learned is that authenticity is not about being perfect. It is about being real. It is about accepting yourself fully and allowing others to see you for who you are, flaws and all.

I am still on this journey, but every day I choose to live in alignment with my truth. I trust my voice, honor my needs, and let go of the need to be anyone other than myself. It is not always easy, but it is always worth it. Because at the end of the day, a life lived authentically is the only life that truly belongs to you.

Overcoming Barriers to Authenticity: Breaking Free from the Bullshit

Embracing authenticity is not a walk in the park. It is more like hiking up a steep, rocky trail with a backpack full of other people's expectations and your own self-doubt weighing you down. The path is not always smooth, and the obstacles are plenty. But here is the truth. Every step you take toward living authentically is a step toward freedom, self-respect, and a life that actually feels like yours.

The biggest barriers to authenticity come from two places. The voices inside your head that tell you who you should be, and the world around you that reinforces those messages. The internal struggles are the ones that whisper (or scream) doubts, fears, and insecurities. They tell you to stay small, play it safe, and avoid rocking the boat. The external pressures come from society, culture, family, and even well-meaning friends who think they know what is best for you. They push expectations onto you, often without even realizing they are doing it.

Living authentically means cutting through all that noise. It means peeling back layers of conditioning and outdated beliefs, questioning what you have been taught, and deciding for yourself who you really are. It is not easy. But neither is living a life where you constantly feel like you are performing instead of actually *being*.

Authenticity takes courage. It takes resilience. It takes the willingness to be misunderstood, judged, or even rejected by those who do not get it. But the reward is a life that feels honest, aligned, and deeply fulfilling. A life where you can finally breathe, knowing you are no longer twisting yourself into shapes to fit someone else's expectations.

The road to authenticity is not about arriving at some perfect, fully enlightened version of yourself. It is about continuously choosing to be real, even when it is uncomfortable. It is about trusting yourself enough to show up as you are, flaws and all, and knowing that who you are is *enough*.

Societal Pressures: The Silent Puppet Master

Societal pressures are sneaky as hell. They do not always scream in your face. Sometimes, they whisper in the background, subtly convincing you that you need to be, act, or look a certain way to be worthy. These pressures come from every direction. Family, culture, media, and even the people you surround yourself with all carry their own definition of what it means to be acceptable, successful, or desirable. Before you even realize it, you are contorting yourself into a version of someone you barely recognize just to meet an invisible standard that keeps shifting.

The real challenge is learning how to separate the noise from the truth. It is about stepping back and asking yourself if this is something you actually believe or if it is something you have been conditioned to believe. Because when we prioritize what society expects over our own inner truth, we end up losing the most important thing. Ourselves.

The Price of Trying to Fit In

For me, societal pressures did not just influence my decisions. They damn near consumed me. As a teenager, my self-image and self-worth were completely hijacked by the standards set by the modeling, pageant, and acting worlds I was immersed in. These industries had a clear message. Your success is directly tied to how thin you are. And if you were not thin enough, good luck trying to be seen.

This was the early nineties, the peak of the waif-thin obsession. Think Kate Moss, heroin chic, and the idea that the less space you occupied, the more valuable you were. Everywhere I looked, the same message was drilled into me. The thinner you are, the more opportunities you get. The more acceptable you are. The more desirable you become. And I bought into it, hook, line, and sinker.

At first, it was subtle. Skipping meals here and there, obsessing over every calorie, I would run for hours, come home and do sit-ups with my feet under the couch and then pass out with exhaustion. But it did not take long before this so-called discipline spiraled into a full-blown eating disorder. Anorexia became my way of gaining control in a world that made me feel powerless. I convinced myself that as long as I could control my weight, I could control my worth. And that was the biggest lie I ever told myself.

When Beauty Becomes a Battle

I was not just struggling with an eating disorder. I was battling a deep-rooted belief that my entire value as a human being depended on a number on a scale. I would look in the mirror and never see someone good enough, no matter how much weight I lost. I became anemic, exhausted, and constantly dizzy, but I still believed I was not small enough. My body was screaming for help, and I ignored it because in my mind, nothing mattered more than being thin.

Then, at eighteen, everything changed. I found out I was pregnant with my first child.

Most women in that moment feel joy, excitement, maybe even a little fear about becoming a mother. Me? I was terrified, but not of motherhood. I was terrified of gaining weight.

Let that sink in.

Instead of feeling overwhelmed with love for the life growing inside me, I was consumed with panic about how my body was about to change. My eating disorder did not just vanish because I was carrying a baby. If anything, it latched on tighter. I continued starving myself, desperate to keep my body as small as possible, as if my worth depended on it.

At my six-month checkup, I weighed only one hundred sixteen pounds. I was hiding my pregnancy so well that people barely noticed. I wore tight clothes that compressed my stomach, clinging to the illusion of a flat abdomen. I was not just harming myself anymore. I was putting my baby's life in danger, and deep down, I knew it.

My doctor saw it too. At that checkup, he did not sugarcoat anything. He laid it out in the bluntest terms possible. I was not just risking my own health. I was risking my child's. I was starving my baby. I was playing a dangerous game, and if I did not stop, there would be serious consequences.

That conversation was my wake-up call.

And let me tell you, I *took* that advice. I took it and ran with it like I had just been told I had an all-access pass to a buffet. After years of restricting, it was like a dam burst, and I ate everything in sight. I went from barely eating to devouring food like I was making up for lost time. By the time I had my son, I had gained so much weight that I went from a size two to a size fourteen. My body expanded so fast that I ended up with stretch marks from my belly button down. And just like that, my lifelong body image issues decided to throw a damn sequel.

Losing the weight was not some cute little fitness journey where I discovered self-love and easily dropped the pounds. It took years. Years of struggling, crying in dressing rooms, feeling like a stranger in my own skin, and trying to find confidence when all I saw was someone I did not recognize. It was emotionally brutal. Even now, my stretch marks remain one of my biggest insecurities. I avoid looking at them too long because they remind me of just how hard that chapter of my life was.

But in the moments when body image issues creep in, I remind myself of the truth. My body was the vessel that brought two incredible souls into this world. That is beautiful. That is strength. And even though my brain loves to be a petty little gremlin about my scars, the reality is that this body has done some miraculous things.

Reclaiming My Worth

Breaking free from the grip of anorexia was not easy, and it did not happen all at once. It took years of unlearning the toxic messages I had internalized. It took therapy, self-reflection, and an entirely new way of looking at my body. It took learning that my worth had nothing to do with my weight and everything to do with the person I was.

Looking back, I see how much societal pressures distorted my perception of beauty, success, and self-worth. It took time, healing, and a whole lot of self-reflection to understand that my value does not come from my size. True beauty has nothing to do with how much you weigh. It comes from within. It is found in the way you live, love, and show up in the world as your truest self.

I share this part of my journey because I know I am not the only one who has been caught in this trap. So many people feel pressured to live up to unrealistic and damaging standards. My hope is that by speaking openly about my experience, someone else might see that they are not alone.

It is hard work to break free from societal pressures, but it is work worth doing. The first step is recognizing that your value does not come from how you look. It comes from who you are. Surround yourself with people who see you for your soul, not your appearance. Learn to love and accept yourself, flaws and all. Choose to live a life that honors your health, your well-being, and your authentic self.

Because the moment you stop trying to fit into society's mold is the moment you finally start living for *you*.

Fear: That Annoying Voice That Won't Shut Up!

Fear is the loudmouth in your head that never knows when to shut up. It is the biggest roadblock on the path to authenticity, always lurking around, whispering bullshit like *What if they judge you? What if you fail? What if you are not enough?* Fear thrives on keeping you small, making you believe that being your true self is risky. And let's be real, sometimes it is. Because the world is full of people who love to judge, and society has a habit of shaming those who do not fit into its neat little boxes.

I spent years playing a role that was not really me. Fear had me in a chokehold, convincing me that if I was honest about who I was and what I had been through, I would never be taken seriously. That if people knew the full story, the addiction, the stripping, the self-destruction, they would write me off as some lost cause who had no business building a life worth being proud of.

But here is the truth. Fear is a liar. Fear is a manipulative little shit that feeds on your insecurities and past trauma. It tells you that playing it safe is the way to go, that shrinking yourself down to fit in is better than standing out. But playing small never did a damn thing for me except keep me stuck in cycles of self-sabotage.

Fear kept me drinking, snorting, and numbing myself until I barely recognized the person staring back at me. It kept me in toxic relationships where I was more focused on being loved by the wrong people than respecting myself enough to walk away. It made me doubt every single move I made, making me feel like I was one misstep away from being exposed as a fraud.

But here is what I learned. You cannot wait for fear to disappear before you start living authentically. Because it never goes away completely. The only way to shut it up is to push through it. To show up as you are, flaws and all, and decide that you are done living according to what other people think is acceptable.

Embracing authenticity is not a one-and-done deal. It is a commitment. It is a daily decision to say, *screw it, this is me* and keep moving forward, even when fear tries to pull you back. Because the more you lean into who you truly are, the less power fear has. And let's be honest, wouldn't it be nice to finally live a life that feels like yours instead of a performance for everyone else?

And here's the wild part—once you start choosing authenticity over approval, something shifts. The people who were only in your life because you were pretending start to fall away, and the ones who see and love the *real* you begin to show up. You start attracting opportunities that align with your truth, not your façade. Life gets messier, yes—but also more meaningful. Because when you finally stop editing yourself to be palatable, you make room for real connection, real purpose, and a version of freedom that fear can't touch.

Self-Doubt: That Nagging Little Asshole in Your Head

If fear is the loudmouth, self-doubt is the passive-aggressive little asshole that keeps poking you in the ribs. It makes you question your worth, your abilities, and whether you even have the right to take up space. It makes you overthink every decision, every word, and every step forward. It is that voice that says, *who do you think you are?*, when you dare to dream bigger for yourself.

I know self-doubt intimately. It lived rent-free in my head for years, telling me that I was never going to be more than the girl who had a past full of mistakes and regrets. It convinced me that because I had spiraled so deep into addiction, I was unworthy of anything better. It made me believe that I had to prove myself over and over just to be *allowed* to have a seat at the table.

When I left the world of exotic dancing and stepped into advanced aesthetics, spiritual coaching, and building Skull Sugar Cosmetics, self-doubt was waiting for me at every corner. It told me I had no business helping others, that my past disqualified me from ever being respected. It whispered that I was an imposter, that sooner or later, someone would call me out and expose me as a fraud.

But here is what I have come to realize. Self-doubt is a liar just like fear, and the only way to shut it down is to stop entertaining it.

You do not need permission to be successful. You do not need validation to step into your power. And you sure as hell do not need to be perfect to be worthy.

The truth is my past is not something that disqualifies me. It is the very thing that makes me damn good at what I do. Because I get it. I understand struggle. I know what it feels like to hit rock bottom and claw my way back up. I know what it means to fight for myself when every part of me wanted to give up. And that makes me more qualified than any textbook ever could.

Overcoming self-doubt is not about never feeling it again. It is about calling it out on its bullshit and refusing to let it control you. It is about deciding that you are enough right now, not when you reach some imaginary level of success, not when you feel completely confident, but *right now*.

So, every time self-doubt tries to creep in and convince you that you are not good enough, remind yourself of this. You do not need to be perfect. You just need to be *real*. And that is more than enough.

Cultural Norms and Traditions: The Unwritten Rulebook of Conformity

Cultural norms and traditions are like that overbearing relative at family gatherings who has an opinion on everything. They dictate what is considered acceptable, respectable, and appropriate, shaping everything from career choices to emotional expression to the way we dress. They can be meaningful, rich in history, and even grounding. But they can also be suffocating as hell when they force you into a mold that has nothing to do with who you actually are.

Many cultures carry unspoken rules about gender roles, career paths, or family obligations. These expectations are deeply ingrained, passed down like some sacred heirloom that you are just supposed to accept without question. And if you do question them? If you dare to carve your own path? Cue the side-eyes, the guilt trips, and the inevitable *You are going to regret this one-day* lectures from people who think they know your life better than you do.

When these expectations clash with who you really are, it creates an internal battle. You might feel like you are being pulled in two different directions. The life you want versus the life that has been laid out for you. And let me tell you, that dissonance is exhausting. It chips away at your identity, making you feel like a stranger in your own skin.

But here's the truth—they don't have to understand your path for it to be valid. Breaking away from tradition doesn't mean you're disrespecting your roots; it means you're choosing to grow in your own direction. You can honor where you came from without sacrificing who you're becoming. The real rebellion isn't loud or angry—it's quietly, boldly becoming exactly who you were always meant to be, even if it makes a few people uncomfortable.

Family Expectations: The Guilt-Laden Chain of Obligation

Ah, family expectations. The original societal pressure cooker. From a young age, many of us are spoon-fed ideas of what success looks like, what happiness should be, and what paths are acceptable. Whether it is career choices, religious beliefs, or even who you are supposed to marry, families often have a very clear vision of the life they expect you to live. And while this usually comes from a place of love, it can also feel like you are carrying a weight that was never yours to bear.

Let's be real. The fear of disappointing family can push you into decisions that have nothing to do with what you actually want. You might marry someone because it keeps the peace. You might pursue a career that makes them proud but makes you miserable. You might stay silent about your real thoughts, beliefs, or identity just to avoid the backlash of stepping outside their expectations.

Speaking from my experience, family expectations can completely derail the life you want to live. I know this all too well because, at sixteen, those expectations led me straight into a marriage I was not ready for.

My mother was convinced this marriage was the best thing for me. Maybe she thought it would give me a better life than she had. Maybe she believed stability could only come through marriage. Or maybe she just did not know what else to do with me. Whatever her reasoning, I was not given much of a choice.

I was a teenager. I wanted to go to prom, date, and just be a normal kid. But that was not in the cards for me. Instead of planning my future, I was preparing for a wedding. At first, I thought I was in love. Looking back, I realize I was just a kid who had no clue what love even was. As the wedding day got closer, panic started setting in. I knew this was not what I wanted. I begged my mother to let me call it off. She refused. Instead, she shipped me off to live with my aunt and uncle in Washington until the wedding, as if distance would make me stop questioning it.

The day of the wedding came, and I could barely breathe. I was walking down the aisle, heart racing, hyperventilating so badly I thought I might pass out. Every step felt like I was marching toward a life that did not belong to me. My brain was screaming, *Someone object. Someone stop this. Please, someone say something.* But no one did. I made it down that aisle, said the vows, and just like that, I was married.

You would think marriage would come with a fresh start, but let me tell you, this one came with a whole new set of problems. The night before our wedding, my husband got drunk and wrecked our car, leaving us with a financial disaster before we even started our life together. And because he was in the Navy and still living in the barracks, our first few months of marriage involved me crashing at his friend's house. The whole thing was a mess.

It only took six months before he was deployed to Japan, and it did not take long for the cheating to start. I would later find out that not only had he been unfaithful, but he had also proposed to someone else while still being married to me. And just to add an extra layer of betrayal, his mistress had been a guest at our wedding, we went to school together...she was his "Best Friend", and boy did she ever hate me! And now I know why. Back then I was always confused as to how someone who barely knew me could carry such disdain for me. But once I learned the cold hard truth, it all made perfect fucking sense!

The final straw came when I opened a phone bill for nine thousand dollars. He had been calling her from Japan on my dime. I called the number, and sure enough, her mom answered, she told me that her daughter and my husband had always had a secret relationship. Wow, and she did not even think to stand up an object to that wedding?! That phone call confirmed what I already knew. This marriage had never been real to him. He had never been faithful. And I was nothing more than an obstacle in whatever life he was trying to live. I felt like nothing more than the trophy he showed off to his Navy buddies at the parties we went to, but she was the one he wanted to have babies with. (And they did, 6 of them to be exact!)

What made it even worse was that during this time, I suffered a miscarriage. I almost bled to death. I lost so much blood that they had to perform an emergency D&C. When I woke up from surgery, I expected to see my husband by my side. Instead, he had gone to see *her*. I was alone, in pain, and finally realizing that I had been abandoned long before I ever signed those marriage papers.

Even though I had never wanted that marriage, the betrayal still cut deep. It was not just about him. It was about the fact that I had been pushed into something I never wanted in the first place. I had begged not to do this, and yet, there I was, picking up the pieces of a life that had never been mine to begin with.

When the divorce was final, I had no choice but to move back in with my parents. Talk about full-circle misery. The very people who had forced me into that marriage now watched as I returned home, broken, humiliated, and feeling like I had lost every bit of control over my own life. It took years to undo the damage that experience left behind.

That marriage taught me a brutal lesson. When you let others dictate your life, you are the one who pays the price. When you silence your own voice to please everyone else, you end up losing yourself in the process.

Looking back, I still feel the weight of what happened. But I also see the strength it took to break free. That experience shaped the way I see family expectations, love, and most importantly, my own worth. I learned that I do not owe anyone my life, my choices, or my future. And neither do you.

If you are feeling trapped by what your family expects of you, hear me when I say this. You are the one who must live with your decisions. Not them. Not your parents. Not your culture. You. And the moment you start living for yourself instead of for their approval, that is the moment you truly start living.

Peer Influence and Social Comparison: The Never-Ending Mind Game

Peer influence and social comparison are like the toxic best friends of conformity. They push you to fit in, tone yourself down, and, in some cases, completely vanish into the crowd. Whether it is in school, at work, or within your social circles, the pressure to be accepted can feel like a relentless game where the rules are always changing. You start nodding along to opinions that do not match yours, laughing at jokes that are not funny, and tucking away the parts of yourself that might get a raised eyebrow or a side-eye from the wrong person.

And then, there is the absolute mind warp that is social media. If peer pressure in real life is bad, social media takes it to an entirely new level. Scroll through those curated, perfectly filtered lives for too long, and suddenly, your existence starts to feel like a half-baked attempt at being a real adult. The vacations, the flawless skin, the engagements, the designer outfits, the happy couples who somehow never have morning breath—before you know it, you are convinced you are failing at life.

It is all smoke and mirrors. Nobody is as perfect as they make themselves look online, but that does not stop people from falling into the trap of measuring their worth against someone else's highlight reel. And the worst part? The moment you start chasing that illusion of perfection, your true self gets left in the dust.

Stop Playing the Comparison Game and Start Owning Who You Are

Living authentically means stepping out of this exhausting cycle of comparison and embracing exactly who you are, no filters, no pretenses.

It means resisting the urge to shrink yourself down into someone else's idea of perfection and instead celebrating the wild, beautiful, and completely unpolished reality of your own life.

I will never forget a vacation I took to Mexico. My partner and I were sitting at a restaurant, enjoying our food and soaking in the moment, when we noticed a family at the next table. They were dressed to the nines, looking like they had just stepped off the pages of a luxury travel magazine. Every detail was perfect, from their coordinated outfits to their effortless smiles. But something was off.

It took about five seconds to realize they were not actually on vacation. They were on a full-blown content creation mission. Snap, pose, repeat. The wife was glued to her phone, strategically placing her sunglasses, angling her drink just right, and making sure every shot was social media gold. Meanwhile, her husband wrangled the kids, making sure they were fed, entertained, and, most importantly, kept out of the shot unless they were needed for a family photo.

Not once did she acknowledge her family. Not once did she put the phone down and just *be* in the moment with them. It was all for the gram.

This is not about judging how anyone lives their life, but let me tell you, that moment was a gut-check reminder of what really matters. I thought about all the times I have laughed with my kids until my stomach hurt, all the spontaneous, ridiculous, messy, beautiful moments we have shared. And I realized something.

None of it was ever staged. None of it was curated. And none of it needed to be broadcast to prove it was real.

There is nothing wrong with sharing your life online, but if you are living for the likes instead of the moment, that is when you need to take a step back. The magic is not in what looks perfect to the outside world. It is in the unfiltered, chaotic, wonderful reality that you actually get to live.

Social Institutions and Structural Expectations: The Unwritten Rulebook for Fitting In

Social institutions like schools, workplaces, and religious organizations act as society's gatekeepers, setting the standards for what is considered acceptable. They dictate how we should think, behave, and measure success, whether we agree with them or not. Schools push specific career paths as the "right" ones, workplaces have silent dress codes and behavioral norms, and religious institutions often come with strict guidelines on how life should be lived. Step outside of those expectations and suddenly you are the problem, the black sheep, the one who just does not get it.

The pressure to conform is relentless. If you are not careful, you will find yourself trying to fit into a system that does not actually align with who you are. The battle between what you are supposed to do and what actually makes your soul happy can be exhausting, leaving you questioning whether you are making choices for yourself or for everyone else.

The Impact of Societal Pressures: Living on Autopilot

The weight of these expectations can make authenticity feel like an impossible luxury. You check the right boxes—career, relationships, stability—but something still feels off. It is like wearing a perfectly tailored suit that somehow feels two sizes too small.

When society pushes everyone to follow the same blueprint for success, it strips away individuality. People trade their quirks, creativity, and messy brilliance for a polished, socially acceptable version of themselves.

And for what? To fit into a mold that was never meant to hold them? The world does not need more people blindly following the rules. It needs people who are willing to tear up the script and rewrite their own damn story.

Overcoming Societal Pressures: The Ultimate Rebellion

Breaking free from these expectations takes guts. It requires questioning ideas that have been shoved down your throat since childhood. But if you want a life that actually feels like yours, you have to start asking the hard questions. Who sets these standards? Are your goals truly yours, or are they borrowed dreams from someone else?

Choosing authenticity means setting boundaries and building the confidence to walk your own path, even if it makes people uncomfortable. Some choices will shake things up. Some conversations will get awkward. But living for yourself instead of for external validation? That is real freedom.

This is Where You Take the Lead

I have shared my struggles, my victories, and the lessons that reshaped me. Now it is your turn. The spotlight is shifting to you, and this is where your journey begins.

The next sections will help you break free from all the noise, tap into your inner wisdom, and start making choices that reflect who you really are. Through guided exercises and reflections, you will begin to uncover the real you—not the version designed to keep everyone else happy, but the one who is unapologetically and undeniably you. Get ready, because things are about to get real.

Exercises: Uncovering Your True Self

Embracing authenticity is not just about peeling back the layers; it is about doing so with a little flair and maybe some well-placed sarcasm to keep things interesting. To help you on this enlightening and occasionally chaotic journey, dive into these journaling prompts and activities. They are designed to push your self-awareness, spark some *Aha!* moments, and maybe even make you laugh at just how absurdly complicated being human can be.

1. Reflect on Moments of Authenticity

Think about a time when you felt completely, unapologetically yourself. No filters, no pretending, no concern about who was watching. What were you doing? Who were you with? How did it feel? What parts of your personality were you expressing? Reflect on what made that experience feel so real and how you can bring more of that energy into your daily life.

2. Identify External Influences

Take a brutally honest look at the expectations society, culture, family, or social circles have placed on you. Which of these influences align with who you are, and which ones feel like a suffocating straitjacket? Write about the areas where you feel pressured to conform and brainstorm ways to give those pressures the middle finger in favor of living more authentically.

3. Explore Your Fears and Doubts

What fears or self-doubts keep you from fully embracing who you are? Are you worried about being judged, rejected, or laughed at? Do you hesitate to be real because you are afraid people will not accept the raw, unpolished version of you? Write down these fears and how they have shaped the way you present yourself to the world. Then, dig into how you can start facing those fears head-on and stepping into your truth with confidence.

4. Define Your Core Values

Grab a notebook and make a list of your core values—the principles that truly matter to you, the ones that shape how you want to live your life. Once you have them written down, take a hard look at how well your current life actually aligns with them. Are you living in a way that honors these values, or are you constantly compromising them to please others? If there are areas where you are out of alignment, write down a game plan for how to get back on track.

5. Visualize Your Authentic Self

Close your eyes and imagine a life where you are fully, unapologetically yourself in every aspect. How do you talk? How do you carry yourself? What kind of work do you do? Who is in your inner circle? What does your day-to-day life look like when you are no longer filtering yourself to fit in? Write it all down and use this vision as a blueprint to start making choices that actually serve *you*.

By engaging in these exercises, you will begin peeling back the layers of conditioning, expectation, and self-doubt that have kept you from fully stepping into your true self. Embracing authenticity is not a one-and-done task—it is an ongoing process that requires self-reflection, courage, and a commitment to living life on your own terms. The more real you allow yourself to be, the more meaningful, fulfilling, and *ridiculously freeing* your life will become.

Chapter 3

Navigating Life's Challenges

"Life is not about dodging the chaos. It is about
learning to laugh when you trip over it, get back up,
and keep going like a badass." —Jamie

Life is a full-contact sport, complete with unexpected plot twists, faceplants, and moments where you question if the universe is just messing with you for fun. One minute, everything is smooth sailing, and the next, you are knee-deep in a mess you never saw coming. That is the reality of being human. Beautifully unpredictable, sometimes frustrating, but always an opportunity to grow.

In this chapter, we are diving headfirst into the art of handling life's curveballs with resilience, a little grit, and enough humor to keep you from spiraling into a full-blown existential crisis. The hard truth is that challenges are unavoidable. Whether it is a minor inconvenience that throws off your day or a soul-crushing moment that makes you question everything, these obstacles are not here to break you. They are here to shape you.

We are going to talk about how to maintain your footing when life yanks the rug out from under you. How to take setbacks, shake off the bullshit, and keep moving forward. How to turn detours into opportunities instead of staring at roadblocks like they are your personal invitation to give up. And most importantly, how to stay true to yourself while navigating all the chaos.

By the time we are through, you will be better equipped to face life's messiest moments with confidence, clarity, and the kind of resilience that makes people wonder what the hell your secret is. So, take a deep breath, roll up your sleeves, and get ready because life is coming whether you are prepared or not. Let's make sure you are.

The Role of Challenges in Growth

Challenges are life's way of saying, "Alright, let's see what you have got." They show up uninvited, usually at the worst possible time, and proceed to shake things up in ways we never saw coming. But here is the kicker. Those moments of chaos, disappointment, and "why me" meltdowns are where the real growth happens.

Nobody wakes up thinking, "You know what would really make today great? A massive personal crisis." We all dream of a smooth ride, a drama-free life where our biggest dilemma is choosing between takeout or cooking something that will probably end up burnt anyway. But life loves to keep things interesting. It throws curveballs like it is getting paid per emotional breakdown, and we either learn how to adapt or we stay stuck.

I have had my fair share of setbacks. Moments where I questioned my strength, my direction, and whether I had it in me to keep pushing forward. Life has knocked me down, flipped my plans upside down, and forced me to rebuild more times than I can count. And as much as I have cursed those moments, I can also say this. Every single one of them made me stronger.

Challenges do not just test us. They teach us. They show us who we really are when things get tough. When the comfort zone disappears, that is when we find out just how much resilience we actually have. I have had to pivot, reassess, and make choices I never thought I would have to make. And while none of it was easy, it shaped me into the person I am today.

The truth is challenges force us to grow. They push us out of the routines that keep us stuck and into the uncomfortable but necessary space of transformation. And let's be honest. Some of the hardest moments in life also come with the best stories. That breakup that crushed you. That career shift that felt like a failure. That time you thought everything was falling apart, only to realize later that it was falling into place. Those are the moments that define you.

So, as we dig into this chapter, let's reframe challenges for what they really are. Opportunities to level up. They are not fun, they are not easy, but they are necessary. Because the truth is, nothing worth having comes from staying the same. Growth requires discomfort, resilience, and a little bit of faith that, in the end, you will come out stronger than you ever thought possible.

Resilience and Empowerment

Building resilience and stepping into your power is like becoming a badass warrior—minus the sword and battle armor, but with the battle scars to prove you have been through some shit and come out stronger. Resilience is not about avoiding hardship; it is about taking the hits, standing back up, and saying, "That all you got?" It is about rolling with the punches, learning from every fall, and refusing to let life's inevitable sucker punches define you.

Empowerment is knowing you are the one in charge of your story, no matter how many plot twists life throws at you. It is realizing you are not just a character in someone else's script; you are the damn author. It is about owning your power, even when everything feels like a chaotic mess, and recognizing that you get to decide how the next chapter plays out. Sure, you cannot control every obstacle, but you can control how you handle them, and that is where true strength lies.

So, how do you build that kind of resilience and keep that fire of empowerment burning, even when life is handing you a dumpster fire instead of a fairytale? First, you have to shift your mindset. Instead of seeing challenges as roadblocks, start seeing them as detours leading you somewhere better. Every setback, every disappointment, every "what the hell just happened" moment is an opportunity to grow, adapt, and become even stronger. The key is not letting those moments break you—it is letting them refine you.

Then, there is self-compassion. You would not berate your best friend for making a mistake, so why the hell do it to yourself? Give yourself grace. Let yourself be human. You are allowed to mess up, to struggle, and to take time to figure things out. The real power comes when you acknowledge where you are, without shame, and still choose to keep going.

Let's talk about your circle. The people you surround yourself with can either be your biggest source of strength or the dead weight holding you back. Keep the ones who lift you up, remind you of your worth, and will sit with you in the trenches when shit hits the fan. Cut loose the ones who drain your energy, make you feel small, or guilt-trip you into living a life that is not yours. Empowerment thrives in spaces where you are supported, not suffocated.

And let's not forget the magic of saying no. Boundaries are not just a cute self-care buzzword—they are necessary. Protecting your energy, time, and emotional well-being is not selfish; it is survival. If something or someone is draining you more than fueling you, it is okay to step back. It is okay to say, "Not today, Satan," and walk away from anything that does not serve your growth.

Now, if there is one thing that has saved me more times than I can count, it is humor. Life will test you, sometimes in ways that feel downright cruel. But if you can laugh—even through the tears—you have already won half the battle. Finding the ridiculousness in a shitty situation does not mean you are ignoring the pain; it means you are refusing to let it consume you. Laughter keeps you from spiraling, keeps things in perspective, and reminds you that no matter how bad things get, you are still here, still standing, and still capable of joy.

And finally, resilience and empowerment are built through persistence. It is about showing up for yourself, even when you do not feel like it. It is about getting up every day and deciding that no matter what happened yesterday, you are going to keep moving forward. Not because someone else expects it, but because you damn well deserve a life that feels good to you.

So, whether you are facing heartbreak, career struggles, personal battles, or just the everyday grind of being a human in a chaotic world, remember this: resilience is not about being invincible. It is about being unbreakable in your determination to keep going. And empowerment? That is just you stepping into your own damn power, refusing to let anyone—including yourself—dim your light. You are the warrior in your own story. Own it.

1. Embrace Your Inner Optimist, Even If They Are Hiding

Let's be honest. When life throws challenges your way, it is easy to slip into a cycle of negativity. The weight of problems can feel suffocating, making it seem like you are carrying the entire world on your back with no relief in sight. Before you give in to doom and gloom, take a deep breath and call on your inner optimist. Even if they have been buried under layers of doubt, they are still there, waiting to help you shift your mindset in a way that makes life feel a little lighter.

Optimism does not mean plastering on a fake smile and pretending everything is perfect. It is about intentionally choosing to focus on what is still good in your life, even when it feels like everything is unraveling. Instead of getting lost in all that is going wrong, challenge yourself to find at least one thing that is going right. Maybe it is the warm cup of coffee that hit the spot this morning, a short but meaningful conversation with a friend, or the small but mighty victory of making it through the day without misplacing your keys.

By concentrating on these positive moments, no matter how small, you create a foundation of resilience. Imagine stacking stones one by one to build a strong and steady base. Each positive thought you cultivate adds to your inner strength, making it easier to withstand whatever storm may come your way. This approach does not just improve your mood in the moment. It also transforms the way you tackle obstacles. The more you acknowledge the little things that are working in your favor, the more you start to believe that bigger and better days are ahead.

Optimism is not about denying hardships. It is about recognizing that, yes, life can be tough, but this moment is not the final chapter. It is about holding onto hope, knowing that brighter days are on the horizon, and trusting that you have the strength and resources to move forward one step at a time. Even when today feels overwhelming, tomorrow holds the possibility of another great cup of coffee, an easier day, and maybe even a few fewer frustrations.

So, the next time life tests you, resist the urge to let negativity take over. Instead, lean into that inner optimist and begin stacking those small victories. You may find that even the toughest days become a little easier when you choose to recognize the good, no matter how small it may seem.

2. Build Your Support Squad

Every superhero needs a strong team, and when it comes to resilience, your support squad is everything. These are the people who cheer you on, remind you of your strengths, and offer comfort when you need it most. Your support system is not just there for the celebrations and easy moments. They are the ones who stand beside you when life feels uncertain, helping you regain your footing when the ground beneath you starts to feel shaky.

Surround yourself with friends, family members, or even that one coworker who always shares the best memes. These people are your allies on this journey. They are the ones who truly know your story, understand your struggles, and stand by you even when you are struggling to believe in yourself. They celebrate your wins, no matter how small, and offer words of encouragement when you are running on empty.

Do not be afraid to lean on them when times get tough. It is tempting to believe that asking for help is a sign of weakness, but the truth is that resilience is not about carrying every burden alone. It is about recognizing when you need support and having the courage to reach out for it. Your support squad exists to help you carry the load, to remind you that you are not facing life's challenges on your own.

Even the strongest heroes have someone in their corner. Think about Batman. He had Alfred, who offered wisdom, guidance, and a much-needed reality check when necessary. Your support system plays the same role. They help keep you grounded, focused, and strong, even in the most difficult moments. They are your reality check, your cheerleaders, and your sounding board all wrapped up in one.

At the end of the day, resilience is not just about individual strength. It is about the connections we nurture and the people we surround ourselves with. Your support squad is an essential part of your resilience toolkit, helping you navigate life's ups and downs with grace, humor, and the reassurance that you are never truly alone. So, value those relationships, invest in them, and do not hesitate to call on your team when you need them. They have your back, just like you would have theirs.

3. Practice the Art of Letting Go

Empowerment is deeply connected to control, specifically the realization that some things are in your hands while others are not. Imagine gripping a rope in a tug-of-war game that you will never win. The harder you pull, the more exhausted and frustrated you become. Sometimes, the strongest move you can make is to let go of that rope, walk away, and accept that not every battle is meant to be fought.

Whether it is a situation beyond your control, a relationship that drains your energy, or that one sock that mysteriously disappears in every load of laundry, there is power in choosing to let go. By releasing the things that no longer serve you, you create space for what truly matters. This does not mean giving up. It means directing your energy toward what actually moves you forward instead of what keeps you stuck.

When you let go of the need to control everything, you open yourself up to new possibilities and perspectives. You start to understand that some things are simply out of your hands, and that is perfectly okay. Trust that life has a way of unfolding in ways that may not align with your plans but will ultimately lead you where you are meant to go. Letting go is an act of faith. It is faith in yourself, faith in the process, and faith in the idea that surrendering control can be one of the most powerful choices you make.

This is not about passivity. It is about becoming more intentional with your energy. Instead of trying to micromanage every aspect of your life, focus on what you can change—your responses, your choices, and your mindset. By loosening your grip on the uncontrollable, you give yourself the freedom to live with less stress and more clarity.

So, the next time you find yourself clinging to something that is out of your control, take a deep breath and loosen your grip. In doing so, you reclaim your power, free up your energy, and create space for what truly deserves your attention.

4. Laugh in the Face of Adversity

There is a reason people say laughter is the best medicine. When life throws challenges your way, humor can be a game-changer. Finding reasons to laugh does not mean you are ignoring reality. It simply means you are not letting difficulties consume you. Humor provides a fresh perspective, making even the heaviest situations feel a little lighter.

Whether it is watching a comedy that makes you laugh until you cry, swapping jokes with a friend, or chuckling at the absurdity of life's unpredictable twists, do not underestimate the power of humor. It gives you a mental break, offering relief from the weight of stress and frustration.

Laughter creates connection. Sharing a laugh with someone reminds you that you are not alone, even in tough times. Humor has a way of cutting through tension, turning overwhelming moments into manageable ones.

And sometimes, all you can do is laugh. When life seems determined to test you, laughter is a way to take back control. It is a refusal to be defeated, a declaration that no matter what happens, you are still standing.

So, when you are having a rough day, find reasons to laugh. Watch something funny, call a friend, or simply laugh at life's ridiculousness. That simple act of joy strengthens your resilience and reminds you that even in the toughest moments, you can still find reasons to smile.

5. Keep Moving Forward, Even If It Is Just Baby Steps

Resilience is not about bouncing back instantly. It is about taking small, steady steps forward, even when progress feels slow. Some days, those steps may be tiny, like getting out of bed or responding to an overdue message. Other days, they may be bigger, like making a difficult decision or taking a leap toward a new opportunity.

Each small step adds up over time. No matter how slow the progress feels, keep moving forward. Before you know it, you will look back and realize just how far you have come.

By embracing these techniques, you build a resilience toolkit that helps you navigate life's storms while still thriving. So go ahead, channel your inner superhero, and remind yourself that you have got this, cape or no cape.

Chapter 4

Cultivating Inner Peace

*"Inner peace is not the absence of chaos, but the quiet
strength to remain calm in the midst of it, nurturing
a stillness that cannot be shaken by the storms of life."*
—Jamie

Inner Peace is Not About Avoiding the Shitstorm. It is About Standing Strong in the Middle of It.

Let's be honest. Cultivating inner peace in a world that seems to run on stress, deadlines, and unexpected bullshit is no small task. It is like trying to meditate in the middle of a construction zone where the jackhammers are your to-do list, the car alarms are your endless notifications, and the guy screaming in the distance is just life doing its thing. But here is the kicker. Inner peace is not about waiting for the noise to stop. It is about learning how to stay calm and grounded even when everything around you is losing its damn mind.

If inner peace had a physical form, it would be that one unbothered person in a chaotic coffee shop, sipping their latte, completely unshaken by the disaster unfolding around them. It is the ability to find stillness inside yourself no matter what kind of chaos is happening outside. It is about becoming the eye of the hurricane instead of getting tossed around like a plastic bag in the wind.

Now let's be real. Finding that kind of peace can feel impossible when you are constantly being pulled in a thousand different directions. Work, responsibilities, existential dread about the meaning of life. Yeah, that one sneaks in there too. But here is the thing. Inner peace does not require the world around you to change. It does not care if your inbox is overflowing, if your car just broke down, or if someone cut you off in traffic and flipped you the bird. It is an inside job and the sooner you stop waiting for life to calm down, the sooner you can start building that unshakable peace from within.

The Mindfulness Game

One of the best ways to start cultivating inner peace is through mindfulness. Now before you roll your eyes and think I am about to tell you to sit in silence for hours and think about nothing, let me break it down in a way that makes sense. Mindfulness is just the practice of being fully present in the moment without letting your brain hijack you into a stress spiral.

Imagine sitting on the bank of a river, watching the water flow by. Your thoughts and emotions are like leaves floating on the surface. Some are peaceful, some are straight-up chaotic, and some make you want to set the whole river on fire. But instead of jumping in and trying to control the current, mindfulness teaches you to sit back and watch it all pass by. No chasing, no forcing, no drowning. Just observing. And that little bit of distance is where the peace sneaks in.

Meditation Without the Fluff

People love to overcomplicate meditation, but it is really just the act of giving your brain a break from the constant noise. You do not need incense, a guru, or a Himalayan retreat. You do not even need to sit cross-legged unless you actually like that sort of thing. Meditation can be as simple as closing your eyes for a few minutes, focusing on your breath, and letting everything else fade into the background.

And before you tell me you do not have time for it, let me remind you that if you have time to scroll mindlessly through your phone for twenty minutes, you have time to meditate. You can do it in the car while waiting for your coffee order, in the shower, or even while brushing your teeth. It is not about shutting off your brain. It is about giving it a damn minute to breathe.

Handling Life's Bullshit with Grace

Inner peace is not about pretending everything is fine when it is not. It is about knowing that no matter what happens, you are capable of handling it. Shit will hit the fan. That is a guarantee. But instead of letting it send you into a full-blown meltdown, inner peace allows you to take a deep breath, assess the situation, and respond in a way that does not leave you feeling like an emotional tornado.

This is not some toxic positivity nonsense. It is not about forcing yourself to be grateful when everything is on fire. It is about acknowledging that yes, life can be a mess, but you are not that mess. You are the person navigating through it, learning from it, and coming out the other side with a little more wisdom and maybe a few good stories to tell.

Cut Yourself Some Slack

We hold ourselves to ridiculous standards. We expect to be Zen masters in every situation, to never lose our cool, to always be in control. But let's get real. We are human, which means we are going to have days where we lose our shit, cry in the car, or snap at someone who absolutely deserved it.

Inner peace is not about being perfect. It is about how quickly you can regain your balance when life knocks you on your ass. It is about self-compassion, about recognizing that you are doing your best, and about giving yourself permission to be human. The faster you learn to forgive yourself for not having it all together, the more peace you will find.

Finding Your Sanctuary in the Chaos

This chapter is about building that kind of inner peace, the kind that does not crack under pressure. We are diving into real, practical ways to keep your cool when life decides to test your patience. No fluff, no guru-level enlightenment required. Just real strategies for staying grounded when the world feels like it is spiraling out of control.

So, take a deep breath, grab a metaphorical life raft, and let's start building that unshakable peace. Because in a world that is constantly on the move, mastering the ability to stay calm is one of the most powerful things you can do. Let's get to it.

The Importance of Inner Peace

Inner peace is the foundation of overall well-being, and for a damn good reason. It is the quiet strength that keeps you from losing your shit when life throws curveballs, the steady calm that lets you handle chaos without completely unraveling. When you cultivate inner peace, you create a solid base that allows every other part of your well-being to thrive. Your physical health, your mental clarity, your emotional stability, and your spiritual growth all depend on that foundation. Without it, even the smallest inconveniences can feel like the end of the world, knocking you off balance and making life feel like a never-ending uphill battle.

Inner peace is not some luxury reserved for monks on mountaintops. It is a non-negotiable necessity for living a balanced, fulfilling life. Think of it like the foundation of a house. Without it, everything else becomes shaky, unstable, and ready to crumble at the first sign of trouble. When you nurture inner peace, you create a state of mind that is resilient, centered, and grounded, making it a hell of a lot easier to handle life's inevitable bullshit without completely falling apart.

How Inner Peace Affects Your Life

The connection between inner peace and your overall well-being is deep. It is not just about feeling good. It actually has a major impact on your body, your emotions, your mind, and even your sense of purpose.

Physically, inner peace is a stress killer. Stress is like that toxic ex who refuses to leave you alone, wreaking havoc on your body in ways you do not even realize. When you are constantly on edge, your body pumps out cortisol and other stress hormones that, over time, can lead to serious health problems like high blood pressure, heart disease, and anxiety disorders. Inner peace keeps your system in check, helping you stay balanced instead of running on survival mode all the time. Less stress means better sleep, a stronger immune system, and overall better health.

Emotionally, inner peace keeps you from being a ticking time bomb. It gives you the space to process emotions without letting them control you. When you have that inner stillness, you are less likely to snap at people, spiral into overthinking, or let someone else's bad mood ruin your entire day. You stop letting external circumstances dictate how you feel, and instead, you start living on your own terms. You become the kind of person who handles challenges with grace instead of throwing a fit every time something does not go your way.

Mentally, inner peace is a game-changer. When your mind is at peace, it is not cluttered with worries, distractions, or unnecessary bullshit. You think more clearly, make better decisions, and stay focused without getting caught up in mental chaos. When your brain is not in overdrive, you have more room for creativity, problem-solving, and actually enjoying life instead of just reacting to it.

Spiritually, inner peace is what connects you to something bigger than yourself. Whether you call it intuition, the universe, or just having your shit together, inner peace allows you to tap into a deeper sense of purpose. It helps you make choices that align with what truly matters to you instead of chasing after things that do not actually make you happy. It becomes the compass that guides you toward a life that is not just successful on paper but actually fulfilling on a soul level.

How to Cultivate Inner Peace in a World That Runs on Chaos

Maintaining inner peace is not easy, especially in a world that thrives on distraction and drama. Every day, you are bombarded with notifications, obligations, and pressures that can throw you off balance if you are not careful. That is why inner peace is not something that just happens. It is something you have to actively cultivate.

Practices like mindfulness, meditation, and self-reflection are not just trendy buzzwords. They are tools that help you stay grounded even when everything around you is spinning out of control. Mindfulness keeps you in the present moment instead of worrying about the past or stressing about the future. Meditation quiets the constant noise in your head so you can actually hear yourself think. Self-reflection helps you recognize patterns that are not serving you and make changes before life smacks you in the face with a wake-up call.

The Ripple Effect of Inner Peace

The best part about cultivating inner peace is that it does not just benefit you. It radiates outward and influences everything and everyone around you. When you are at peace with yourself, you are not dumping your stress onto others. You communicate better, you make wiser choices, and you create a more positive environment wherever you go. Your relationships improve, your work becomes more fulfilling, and you stop getting caught up in unnecessary drama.

Inner peace is contagious. When you show up as the calm, grounded person in the room, you inspire others to do the same. You stop feeding into negativity and start being a source of stability for the people around you. Whether you realize it or not, your own peace has the power to create a ripple effect that makes the world just a little less chaotic.

Making Inner Peace a Way of Life

This chapter is all about giving you the tools, techniques, and mindset shifts to help you cultivate and maintain inner peace no matter what life throws at you. Whether you are dealing with everyday stress or navigating major life changes, these strategies will help you build a steady, peaceful center that does not crack under pressure.

At the end of the day, inner peace is not just a goal you check off a list. It is a way of life. It is a daily practice that transforms the way you experience the world. And trust me, once you start living from that place of unshakable calm, there is no going back.

Mindfulness Meditation: Because Your Brain Needs a Damn Break

Alright, let's talk about mindfulness and meditation, the powerhouse duo of not losing your shit when life gets chaotic. If you have ever found yourself spiraling into stress faster than a cat chasing a laser pointer, then these practices might just be your new best friends. And before you roll your eyes and assume this involves sitting cross-legged in a robe chanting "om" for hours, let me stop you right there. This is not about reaching some guru-level enlightenment. It is about giving your overworked, overstimulated brain a damn minute to breathe.

I did not stumble into mindfulness meditation because I thought it would be fun to sit quietly and focus on my breath. No, I was dragged into it by my therapist, Fred, after years of my nervous system going into full fight-or-flight mode anytime something triggered me. And by "triggered," I mean anything that sent my anxiety into overdrive—like conflict, stress, or someone just looking at me the wrong way on a day when I was already on edge. My brain's default response was to either prepare for battle or run like hell. Fred, being the patient soul that he was, introduced me to mindfulness meditation as a way to calm the raging storm inside me. And let me tell you, at first, it felt like trying to teach a squirrel to sit still. But once I actually gave it a shot, it changed everything.

So, What the Hell is Mindfulness Anyway?

Mindfulness is basically the art of paying attention. Not the half-assed kind where you pretend to listen while mentally making a grocery list. I mean actually being fully present, noticing the world around you, and tuning into your own thoughts and feelings without immediately labeling them as "good" or "bad." Think of it as people-watching, but instead of judging strangers at the airport, you are watching your own mind do its weird little dance.

It is about observing your thoughts like they are passing clouds instead of chasing after them like a rabid dog. It is about realizing that just because a thought pops into your head does not mean it deserves to control your entire mood. Whether you are sipping your morning coffee, taking a walk, or just breathing, mindfulness invites you to be fully engaged in the moment instead of mentally time-traveling to past regrets or future worries.

Meditation: The Leash for Your Mental Squirrel

If mindfulness is about being present, meditation is about training your mind to stay there without running off on some wild tangent. Think of your mind as an overexcited puppy that sees a million squirrels at once. Meditation is the leash that gently guides it back every time it tries to dart off into an anxiety spiral. And trust me, your mind will chase after all kinds of squirrels—random worries, embarrassing shit you did ten years ago, tomorrow's to-do list, that weird thing your coworker said. Meditation is not about stopping those thoughts. That is impossible unless you are a robot. It is about learning to notice them, acknowledge them, and then bring your focus back to the present without getting tangled up in the nonsense.

When I first started meditating, I was convinced my brain was broken. I would sit down, close my eyes, and two seconds later, my mind would be sprinting through a greatest-hits reel of stress and distractions. But, Fred assured me that this was normal. The point was not to have a perfectly empty mind. The point was to practice bringing my focus back every time it wandered, like gently leading a toddler away from touching a hot stove. Over time, that practice helped me realize that I was not my thoughts. I was the observer of my thoughts. And that tiny shift? It was everything.

But My Brain is a Caffeinated Hamster on a Wheel

I hear you. If you are thinking, "This all sounds great, but my mind never shuts up," welcome to the club. Mindfulness and meditation are not about achieving perfect Zen on day one. They are about learning to sit with whatever chaos is happening inside your head without letting it run the show. It is a practice, not a destination. Every time you take a deep breath, pause before reacting, or notice your thoughts without getting swept away by them, you are strengthening that inner calm.

And the best part? You do not need some fancy-ass setup to get started. No incense, no special cushions, no Tibetan singing bowls. You can practice mindfulness and meditation anytime, anywhere. Sitting in traffic? Focus on your breath instead of flipping off the guy who just cut you off. Standing in line at the grocery store? Instead of doomscrolling, tune into your senses and actually experience the moment. Lying in bed at night overthinking your entire life? Try a simple body scan meditation to ground yourself. I still struggle at times with this. Don't give up.

The Benefits are Legit

If the idea of inner peace is not enough to sell you, let's talk about the actual science-backed benefits. Regular meditation has been shown to lower stress, reduce anxiety, improve focus, boost the immune system, and even help with emotional regulation. Basically, it is like a mental gym workout that makes your brain stronger and more resilient to life's bullshit. The more you practice, the better you get at handling stress without completely losing your mind.

So, whether you are looking to stop overthinking everything, lower your stress levels, or just find a moment of peace in your nonstop day, mindfulness and meditation are simple but powerful tools. And who knows? You might even start enjoying those quiet moments more than you expected. No mountaintop required.

Mindfulness Exercises: Because Inner Peace is Not Just for Monks

Alright, so you want inner peace, but life keeps throwing bullshit your way. I get it. That is exactly why I am handing you this personal toolkit of mindfulness exercises to help you find some damn calm, even when everything around you is a mess. Think of this as your survival guide for sanity. Whether you are drowning in stress, dealing with one of those days where everything goes wrong, or just trying to take a deep breath without someone asking you for something, these exercises will help you reconnect with that still, steady part of yourself that has been buried under the chaos.

And before you start thinking you need to be some enlightened guru to pull this off, let me stop you right there. You do not need a robe, a chanting circle, or a Himalayan retreat. No mystical nonsense is required. These practices are for *real life*. They are simple, accessible, and designed to fit into your daily routine without making you feel like you have to change your entire personality. If you like incense and soft music, go for it, but if your version of peace involves blasting rock music while journaling with a glass of water in hand, that works too. The goal here is not perfection. It is progress.

We will start with the basics: breathing techniques. Because let's be honest, when life gets overwhelming, half of us forget to do the most basic human function properly. Breathing exercises will help you slow down, pull yourself together, and release all the built-up tension you are probably carrying in your shoulders, jaw, and that one tight spot in your back that never seems to go away. Then, we will move on to mindfulness practices that you can sneak into your day without anyone even noticing. Sipping coffee? Boom. Mindfulness. Taking a walk? Yep. That counts too. Hell, you can even do this stuff while brushing your teeth.

And because life has a twisted sense of humor and loves to hit you with unexpected bullshit, I am also giving you a few emergency peacekeeping techniques for those *oh hell no* moments. Stuck in traffic? Dealing with a conversation that is making you want to scream? Feeling like the world is collapsing around you? I have got you covered with quick, no-nonsense strategies to help you reset before you completely lose your mind.

At the end of the day, this is not about achieving some mythical state of total Zen. It is about having tools to help you navigate the insanity of life without completely losing your cool. So take a deep breath, unclench your jaw, and let's get into it.

Guided Meditation: The Five-Minute Reset

Sometimes life comes at you so hard that you do not even have time to sit and process what the hell just happened. That is where this five-minute meditation comes in.

Find a quiet spot. If the bathroom is the only place where you can be alone, that works too. Sit down, close your eyes, and take a deep breath in through your nose. Hold it for a second, then exhale slowly through your mouth. As you breathe, imagine each inhale filling you with calm and each exhale releasing all the tension that has been building up inside you. Do this for five minutes. That's it. No pressure to clear your mind, no stress about *doing it right*. Just breathe and give yourself a damn break.

Journaling Prompt: What Brings Me Peace?

Grab your journal or whatever scrap of paper you can find and take a moment to reflect. Ask yourself, *what truly brings me peace?* Is it blasting music in your car? Walking in nature? That first sip of coffee in the morning before the world realizes you are awake?

Write it all down. Then go a step further and ask yourself, *how can I bring more of these peaceful moments into my daily life?* This is not about overhauling your entire routine. It is about making small changes that help you feel a little more grounded every day.

Everyday Mindfulness: Sneaking Zen into Your Routine

If you do not have time for a full-blown meditation session, no problem. Here are some quick and easy ways to turn everyday moments into mindfulness exercises.

1. The Mindful Morning Coffee Ritual

Instead of mindlessly chugging your caffeine while scrolling your phone, try actually paying attention to the process. Notice the smell of the coffee grounds, the warmth of the mug, and the taste of that first sip. Give yourself a few minutes to just enjoy it without distractions.

2. The Savoring Snack Attack

Next time you grab a snack, slow down. Really taste it. Notice the texture, the flavor, and the way it feels in your mouth. Turn snack time into a full sensory experience instead of inhaling food like a vacuum. Bonus points if you do not get crumbs all over yourself.

3. The Walking Meditation Without Looking Like a Weirdo

You do not have to shuffle around like a monk to practice mindful walking. Just pay attention to your surroundings. Feel the ground beneath your feet, notice the colors of the trees or buildings, and listen to the sounds around you. If you are in a busy place, tune in to the background noise without getting lost in thought.

4. One-Minute Mindfulness Moments

Stuck waiting for something? Use that time for a quick mindfulness check-in. Instead of reaching for your phone, take a deep breath and notice how your body feels. Bring your focus to the present moment, even if it is just for sixty seconds.

5. The Mindful Shower

Instead of zoning out or mentally scripting your next argument, try actually *experiencing* your shower. Feel the water on your skin, listen to the sound of it hitting the floor, and inhale the scent of your soap. Turn this everyday task into a mini spa moment.

6. The Breath Break

When all else fails, just breathe. Take a deep inhale through your nose, hold it for a second, and slowly exhale through your mouth. Repeat a few times. This one is great because you can do it anywhere. At your desk, in a stressful meeting, or while avoiding awkward small talk.

Journaling Prompts for a Little Self-Reflection

1. Think about a recent situation that completely wrecked your inner peace. How did you react? What could you have done differently?
2. Describe a time when you felt truly calm. What was happening? How can you bring more of that energy into your life?
3. List five things that instantly calm you down. How can you make them a regular part of your routine?
4. Imagine your inner peace as a person. What do they look like? What advice would they give you when you are stressed?
5. What is one habit that consistently messes with your peace? What can you do to change it?
6. Write about a time when you chose to walk away from drama instead of engaging in it. How did it feel?
7. Look around your space. What small changes could you make to create a more peaceful environment?
8. How does humor help you stay grounded? Think of a time when laughter saved you from completely losing it.

Finding Your Calm in the Chaos

Let's be real. Life is never going to stop throwing curveballs. You will still have bad days, stressful moments, and unexpected shitstorms. But what you *can* control is how you respond. These mindfulness exercises are not about becoming some perfectly enlightened being who never gets upset. They are about giving yourself the tools to handle life without completely unraveling.

Some days you will nail it. Other days you will forget all of this and spiral into stress mode. That is fine. The key is to keep coming back to these practices, to remind yourself that peace is something you *create*, not something you wait for. You do not need perfect conditions, a special setting, or a flawless routine. You just need to show up for yourself, take a breath, and keep going.

So here is your reminder. You are allowed to slow down. You are allowed to take up space. And you are allowed to tell life to calm the hell down while you drink your coffee in peace.

Chapter 5

Manifesting Your Soul's Purpose

"To manifest your soul's purpose, you must first listen
to the calling within, then move with unwavering
faith, knowing that every step you take brings you
closer to the life your spirit was born to create."
—Jamie

When I was a teenager, I would drag my blankets outside and sleep under the stars, staring into the vastness of space and fantasizing that I was from another galaxy. I was convinced I had been dropped onto this planet for something *big*. I did not know what it was yet, but I could feel it deep in my bones. There was no way I was just here to exist, to wake up, go to school, get a job, and repeat the cycle until the end. No, I was meant for something more, something powerful, something that would shake shit up. I just had no idea how to get from point A to whatever cosmic calling was waiting for me at point B.

Fast forward a few decades, and here I am—an author, spiritual guide, entrepreneur, and someone who has transformed pain into purpose. But let's be clear, I did not wake up one day with a perfectly laid-out roadmap to my soul's calling. Finding and manifesting your purpose is messy, unpredictable, and full of moments that make you want to scream into the void. It is a wild ride, but when you get even a glimpse of what you are meant to do, nothing compares to the feeling of alignment that comes with it.

This chapter is all about helping *you* uncover what that purpose is and how to actually bring it to life. Because let's be honest, manifesting your soul's purpose is not just about *thinking* really hard about what you want and waiting for the universe to drop it in your lap. It is about action, alignment, and trusting that each step you take is leading you exactly where you need to be. So, grab a notebook, a cup of coffee, or whatever fuels your soul, and let's get to work.

Why Manifesting Your Soul's Purpose Matters

Because Without Purpose, Life Feels Like a Chaotic Dumpster Fire

Without purpose, life feels like you are just floating along, reacting to whatever bullshit the day throws at you. You wake up, go through the motions, and wonder why everything feels so damn *meh*. When you are in alignment with your soul's calling, even the tough days feel like they *mean* something. There is a sense of direction, even if the path is not always clear.

Because Fulfillment is an Inside Job

You can have all the external success in the world, but if you are not living in alignment with what actually *lights you up*, you will always feel like something is missing. Your soul's purpose is what fills that void. It is the thing that makes you wake up feeling *right* in your own skin, like you are actually living instead of just existing.

Because Life Will Test You, and You Need a Reason to Keep Going

Let's not sugarcoat it—life can be a relentless pain in the ass. If you do not have a deeper purpose driving you, the rough patches will knock you flat. But when you are connected to something bigger than yourself, you find a level of resilience that helps you push through even the hardest moments. Purpose gives you *fuel* to keep going.

Because the World Needs What You Have to Offer

Your soul's purpose is not just about *you*. It is about the people you are meant to impact, the change you are meant to create, and the legacy you are meant to leave behind. You are here for a reason, and the more you step into your purpose, the more lives you touch—whether you realize it or not.

Because You Are Here to Evolve, Not Just Survive

Your soul's purpose is not a rigid, one-time discovery. It grows as you grow. The more you lean into it, the more it unfolds. This journey is about continuous expansion, learning, and stepping into the fullest, most authentic version of yourself.

Finding Your Soul's Purpose: Personal Reflection

Before we get into the practical steps of manifesting your purpose, let's take a moment to reflect. Sometimes, the best clues about where you are going come from the moments when you felt most *alive*.

Think Back to a Time When You Felt Completely in Tune with Yourself

Close your eyes and scan through your memories. When was the last time you felt completely *right* in what you were doing? Was it when you were helping someone? Creating something? Speaking your truth? Teaching? Learning?

Journal Prompt: Write about a time when you felt fully aligned with who you are. What were you doing? Who were you with? How did it feel?

Identify the Common Threads

What patterns do you notice? Maybe it was always when you were making people laugh, supporting others, writing, or pushing boundaries. These common threads are *clues* to what sets your soul on fire.

Journal Prompt: What themes do you notice in the moments when you felt most in tune with yourself? What does that say about what truly matters to you?

Recognize the Qualities You Were Expressing

Were you being creative, compassionate, bold, intuitive? The qualities you embody when you feel most alive are a reflection of how your soul wants to *show up* in the world.

Journal Prompt: What qualities were you expressing in those moments? How can you bring more of those qualities into your daily life?

Reflect on What This Means for Your Future

Now that you have some clarity, how do you take the next step? What small shifts can you make to live more in tune with your purpose?

Journal Prompt: What steps can you take to create more moments of alignment with your true self? How can you incorporate the insights from this reflection into your daily life?

Takeaway: Your Purpose is Already Within You

Here is the truth—your soul's purpose is not something you have to *find* like some hidden treasure. It is already inside you, waiting for you to pay attention. The moments when you feel *right*, when you feel *alive*, when you feel like you are exactly where you are meant to be? Those are the breadcrumbs leading you toward your purpose.

It is not about waking up one day with all the answers. It is about trusting that each step, even the messy ones, are taking you exactly where you are meant to be. It is about listening to that deep, undeniable knowing inside you—the one that has been there since you were a kid staring up at the stars, convinced that you were *meant* for something bigger.

Because guess what? You *are*. And it is time to start manifesting it.

Understanding the Concept of a Soul's Purpose

Before you can start manifesting your soul's purpose, you have to understand what the hell it actually is. This concept can feel as elusive as trying to catch smoke with your bare hands, but at its core, your soul's purpose is the unique role you were meant to play in this world. It is not about what looks good on paper or what society expects from you. It is about what *feels right* deep in your bones. It is the thing that makes you feel alive, aligned, and like you are actually *doing* something meaningful rather than just existing.

What is a Soul's Purpose?

A Unique Blueprint: The One-of-a-Kind Roadmap to Your Best Life

Think of your soul's purpose as a blueprint that was designed specifically for *you*. It is a mix of your natural talents, your deepest passions, and the lessons you are meant to learn and teach in this lifetime. Unlike traditional goals that focus on external achievements, your soul's purpose is all about the *why* behind everything you do. It is what brings you that unshakable sense of fulfillment, joy, and meaning, the kind that no paycheck, title, or social media clout can ever replace.

Beyond Career and Success: This is Bigger Than a Job Title

A huge misconception is that your soul's purpose has to be tied to your career. While your work *can* be an extension of your purpose, it is not the whole damn picture. Your soul's purpose weaves through every part of your life—your relationships, personal growth, the way you show up for others, and the impact you leave behind. It is about living authentically and unapologetically as *you*, regardless of external validation.

A Guiding Force: The Built-In Compass You Forgot You Had

When you align with your soul's purpose, life starts to make more sense. There is clarity, motivation, and a sense of direction that keeps you from getting stuck in the endless cycle of "What the hell am I doing with my life?". You stop making decisions based on fear, pressure, or comparison and start moving in a way that feels right. And the best part? You do not have to *force* it. Your purpose naturally unfolds the more you follow your passions, trust your intuition, and stay true to your values.

Soul vs. Ego: How to Tell the Difference Between Your Purpose and Your Bullshit

Ego Wants the Spotlight, Your Soul Wants Fulfillment

One of the biggest hurdles in discovering your soul's purpose is learning to separate it from ego-driven desires. The ego craves external validation. It wants status, approval, and proof that you are *somebody*. It is the part of you that gets caught up in what *looks* successful rather than what *feels* right.

Your soul, on the other hand, does not give a damn about appearances. It is not here to impress people. It is here to *express* who you really are. It is about doing what brings you peace, passion, and purpose, even if it does not come with a flashy title or a six-figure salary.

External Success vs. Internal Fulfillment

Ego-driven desires are all about *getting*—money, recognition, validation. They are fueled by fear, comparison, and a need to prove something. Your soul's purpose, though? It is all about *giving*. It is about contributing, creating, and making a difference in a way that feels natural and fulfilling to you. The ironic part? When you live in alignment with your soul's purpose, external success often follows. But it is a byproduct, not the goal.

How to Tell if You Are Chasing Your Soul's Purpose or Your Ego's Illusions

Ask yourself, how do I feel when I think about this?

If a goal makes you feel *peaceful, excited, and deeply aligned*, it is probably tied to your soul's purpose. If it makes you feel *stressed, competitive, or like you need to prove something*, it is likely an ego-driven pursuit. Learning to recognize this difference can save you years of chasing the wrong things.

Authenticity: The Key to Unlocking Your Purpose

Living Authentically: Quit Trying to Fit into Someone Else's Idea of Success

You cannot manifest your soul's purpose while living life according to someone else's script. Your purpose requires you to be *honest* with yourself about what truly matters to you. That means dropping the expectations society, family, or old versions of yourself have placed on you. It means making choices based on *your* values, even if they do not align with what everyone else thinks you "should" do.

Embracing Your Uniqueness: Stop Hiding the Weird, that is Where Your Magic Is

Your quirks, your passions, your unconventional ideas—those are not flaws, they are road signs pointing you toward your purpose. The things that make you different are the things that make you, *you*. Embracing them will bring you closer to your true path.

Perfection is a Myth, and You Do Not Need it to Find Your Purpose

A lot of people hold back from pursuing their soul's purpose because they think they need to have it all figured out first. Newsflash: *You won't*. Your purpose is not a one-time discovery; it is an evolving journey. The more you explore and allow yourself to *try*, the clearer it will become.

Recognizing the Signs of Your Soul's Purpose

You know that gut feeling, that intuitive nudge, that deep knowing inside you that will not shut up? That is your soul talking. Your purpose is *not* hiding from you. It has been leaving you clues all along. You just need to start paying attention.

Following the Breadcrumbs: Your Intuition is Trying to Tell You Something

Your intuition is like an internal GPS that is constantly recalculating to keep you on track, even when you think you've veered off course. It speaks in whispers, gut feelings, and those little "aha" moments that seem to come out of nowhere. And when you feel drawn to something—whether it's a creative pursuit, a career path, or a cause that lights a fire inside you—it's not some random fluke. It's a nudge from your soul saying, *pay attention, this is important.*

But here's the tricky part: intuition doesn't always come with a flashing neon sign or a step-by-step roadmap. It drops breadcrumbs—little clues, synchronicities, and gut feelings that guide you toward what's meant for you. Maybe you keep seeing the same topic pop up in books, conversations, or social media posts. Maybe you feel a magnetic pull toward a certain type of work, even if it doesn't make logical sense. Or maybe you just *know* something deep down, even when you can't explain why.

Your job isn't to have all the answers—it's to follow the breadcrumbs. Say yes to the things that spark your curiosity, even if they don't seem to fit into a grand plan. Trust that the pieces will come together as you go. Intuition rarely lays out the entire journey in advance, but it will always give you the next right step. When you learn to trust those nudges, life starts unfolding in ways you never could have planned—but exactly as it was meant to.

Look at Your Passions and Recurring Themes

What are the things that make you completely forget to check your phone? The things that pull you in so deeply that hours pass like minutes? What topics could you talk about endlessly without ever running out of things to say? And perhaps most telling—what lessons keep circling back into your life, no matter how many times you think you've mastered them?

These aren't just random interests or coincidences. They're breadcrumbs leading you toward your purpose. Your passions are the things that ignite your soul, and those recurring themes? They're life's way of nudging you toward what you're here to do. If a certain subject, activity, or lesson keeps showing up, it's not by accident—it's because there's something there for you to explore, embrace, and possibly share with the world.

Think of it like this: if life were a mystery novel, these passions and patterns would be the clues. Your job isn't to ignore them or chalk them up to chance. It's to pay attention. To ask yourself *why* these things keep calling to you. To lean in instead of brushing them aside. Because within those themes and interests lies something bigger—your purpose, your mission, or at the very least, the next step on your journey.

So, take a moment. What are the things that light you up? What lessons and experiences have shaped you? Where do you keep finding yourself, over and over again? The answers aren't just interesting—they're your soul's way of saying, *hey, this is important. Let's go deeper.*

Listen to Your Inner Voice: It's Trying to Guide You

The problem isn't that your soul isn't speaking—it's that most people are too distracted to hear it. Between the constant notifications, the endless scrolling, and the noise of everyone else's opinions, your inner voice is probably shouting *and* waving its arms trying to get your attention. But clarity doesn't come from more noise; it comes from making space to actually listen.

If you want to hear your soul's guidance, you have to create moments of stillness. That doesn't mean you have to become a monk or retreat to a mountaintop (unless that's your vibe). It can be as simple as taking five minutes in the morning to sit with your thoughts before reaching for your phone, journaling without censoring yourself, or going for a walk without blasting a podcast. The key is to pause long enough to *listen*—to notice the thoughts and feelings that rise to the surface when the world isn't drowning them out.

Meditation, deep breathing, and journaling are all powerful ways to tune in. But so is simply being present—whether that's watching the sunset without rushing to capture it on your phone, driving in silence instead of cranking up the music, or allowing yourself to just *be* without needing to fill the space with constant stimulation.

Your soul is always whispering (sometimes even screaming), trying to guide you. But if you never stop to listen, you'll keep wondering why you feel lost. The answers are already inside you—you just have to quiet the world long enough to hear them.

The Universe is Always Sending You Signs—Are You Paying Attention?

Ever had one of those moments where something just *clicks*? You were thinking about changing careers, and suddenly you meet someone who opens the perfect door. You keep seeing the same message over and over in different places. These are not random. They are synchronicities—little winks from the universe letting you know you are on the right track.

If you are feeling lost, ask for a sign. Then, stay open to *how* it shows up. It might come as a conversation, a song, a book that falls into your lap at the perfect time. The universe loves to play, but you have to be paying attention to catch the messages.

Your Soul's Purpose is Already Inside You, You Just Have to Start Listening

Finding your soul's purpose is not about searching for something outside of yourself. It is about rediscovering what has been inside you all along. It is in the things that bring you joy, in the moments when you feel *most like yourself*, and in the deep knowing that you are meant for something *bigger*.

You do not need permission. You do not need all the answers. You just need to *start*. Trust that every step you take will bring you closer. Because your purpose? It has been waiting for you this whole time.

Step 1: Listen to the Whispers of Your Soul

Your soul has been speaking to you your entire life. The question is, have you been listening? It does not always come through as a loud, booming voice or a dramatic epiphany. More often, it is a quiet nudge, a moment of inspiration, a deep knowing that pulls at you when you least expect it. The problem is life is *loud*. Between the constant ping of notifications, the never-ending to-do lists, and the general chaos of just existing in this world, those whispers from your soul can get drowned out faster than you can say *existential crisis*. It is like trying to hear a breeze rustling through the trees while standing next to a jet engine.

That is why the first step in uncovering your soul's purpose is learning to *shut up and listen*. And I mean *really* listen. This is not about just hearing what your soul is saying—it is about making space for it in the first place. It is about creating those pockets of silence, those moments of stillness where you can actually tune in and recognize what has been there all along.

The soul rarely hands you a full itinerary. It's more of a breadcrumb trail than a GPS, offering glimpses, not guarantees. You might feel drawn to something without knowing why, or feel pulled to let go of something even when it looks perfect on paper. That's the thing about soul whispers—they don't always make logical sense, but they make deep sense. The kind that resonates in your chest before your mind can catch up.

And here's the kicker: you won't always get immediate clarity. Sometimes, the message is "not this," without an immediate follow-up of "but definitely that." Soul work is not a five-step plan with guaranteed results. It's a sacred unfolding, one intuitive yes at a time. So instead of demanding answers, start honoring the questions. Start trusting the pull, the pause, the pivot. Your soul isn't trying to confuse you—it's trying to guide you. You just have to be brave enough to follow the thread without knowing exactly where it leads.

Journaling can be a powerful tool here. Writing things down forces you to slow your thoughts, to process them in a way that just thinking does not quite accomplish. Ask yourself questions like:

- What am I doing when I feel most alive?
- What drains me and leaves me feeling exhausted?
- What recurring themes show up in my life—both in what excites me and what doesn't?

By taking the time to really notice these patterns, you will start to piece together the puzzle of your soul's purpose. Think of it like being a detective, but instead of solving some crime, you are solving *you*. And the more you tune in, the more obvious it becomes that your soul has been talking to you this entire time—you just needed to listen.

Step 2: Reflect on Your Past Experiences

Your life has been leaving you clues about your soul's purpose since the beginning. Some of these clues come wrapped in moments of pure joy, when everything just *clicked*. Others are hidden in struggles, heartbreaks, and the kind of life lessons that made you question everything. But every single experience—good, bad, and everything in between—has been shaping you for something bigger.

Take a moment and ask yourself: What have been the defining moments of my life? What experiences changed me in a way that I could never go back to who I was before? What lessons have I had to learn the hard way?

Some of your biggest clues are hidden in the moments that were *not* easy. Maybe you have had to navigate loss, addiction, betrayal, or failure. Maybe you have survived things you once thought would break you. But here is the thing—sometimes your greatest pain becomes your greatest purpose. The things that nearly took you out might be the very things that allow you to help others. Maybe your journey was never just about *you*. Maybe it was preparing you to guide, teach, or inspire someone else walking a similar path.

But it is not just about the struggles. Your purpose is also woven into your moments of *pure joy*. The times when you felt completely in your element, like the universe had lined everything up perfectly and you were exactly where you were meant to be. Those moments are showing you something just as important. They are proof of what makes your heart light up, what aligns with your soul, what fills you rather than drains you.

Look at the patterns. What connects the experiences that shaped you the most? Maybe every time you helped someone through a difficult time, you felt a deep sense of fulfillment. Maybe every time you were creating, whether it was art, writing, or music, you felt more like *yourself* than at any other time. Maybe every time you stood up for something you believed in, you felt alive in a way nothing else could replicate.

Write these things down. Connect the dots. Because once you do, you will start to see that your soul's purpose has been forming from the very beginning.

Step 3: Identify Your Core Values

Your soul's purpose is not just about what you *do*—it is about *how* you do it. And at the heart of that is your core values. These are the things that guide your choices, shape your beliefs, and dictate what really matters to you. They are the non-negotiables, the things that, when honored, make you feel in alignment, and when ignored, make you feel lost as hell.

Take some time to figure out what your core values actually are. Think about the moments when you felt truly fulfilled—what values were you living out? Then think about the times you felt off-track, unsettled, or frustrated—what values were being compromised?

Here are some questions to get you started:

- What are the qualities in myself that I value the most?
- What makes me feel most *me*?
- What pisses me off the most when I see it in the world? (Because sometimes what enrages you is a sign of what you are meant to fix.)

Once you have identified your core values, ask yourself *how* they fit into your purpose. If one of your core values is freedom, maybe you are meant to create a life where you are not confined by a traditional job. If your core value is creativity, maybe your purpose is to bring beauty and expression into the world. If your value is compassion, maybe you are meant to help people in some deep, meaningful way.

Living in alignment with your values does not just bring you closer to your soul's purpose—it makes life *feel* right. It is like finding the rhythm you were always meant to move to. And when you do that, you naturally start attracting the opportunities, people, and experiences that align with who you are at your core.

Final Thoughts: Your Soul's Purpose is Already in Motion

If you take anything away from this, let it be this: *You do not have to go out and find your soul's purpose. It is already inside you, waiting for you to uncover it.* Every experience, every lesson, every joy, and every struggle has been shaping you into the person you are meant to be. The key is to *pay attention*.

Start listening to the whispers of your soul. Reflect on where you have been and what has shaped you. Identify the values that make you feel the most alive. And then, start moving in that direction—one step, one choice, one moment at a time.

Because the truth is, you have always known on some level what you are here to do. You just have to trust yourself enough to finally start doing it.

Step 4: Own Your Freaking Gifts and Stop Downplaying Them

Here is the deal. You were not put on this earth to just pay bills and scroll through your phone until bedtime. You have gifts. Unique, weird, wonderful, badass gifts that are *yours* and yours alone. And no, I am not talking about your uncanny ability to pick the slowest checkout line every damn time (although, honestly, that is a skill). I am talking about the things that come so naturally to you that you almost do not even recognize them as gifts because they are just *who you are*.

And yet, most people spend their whole lives downplaying these gifts, brushing them off as "no big deal" while struggling to find their purpose. Spoiler alert: your purpose and your gifts are *deeply* connected. Those things you love doing, the things you are naturally good at, the things people always seem to come to you for? They are neon signs pointing directly at what you are meant to be doing in this world.

What Are Your Gifts? (No, Seriously, Think About It)

Maybe you have a way with words, spinning stories that make people feel seen, heard, and understood. Maybe you are a natural problem-solver, thriving in chaos while everyone else is losing their minds. Maybe you are the person who can walk into a room and instantly put people at ease, creating a space where others feel safe, valued, and accepted.

Or maybe your gifts are more subtle. Maybe you are the friend who always knows exactly what to say when someone is falling apart. Maybe you can see potential in people before they even see it in themselves.

Maybe you have a deep connection to nature, animals, energy, or the unseen forces of the universe that others dismiss but you *know* are real.

These gifts are *not* random. They are not just cute little quirks. They are tools you were given to help you fulfill your purpose.

So here is your first assignment: Start paying attention to what people always compliment you on or seek you out for. Not just the shallow stuff like "Oh my God, I love your outfit" (although, let's be real, your fashion sense *is* impeccable). I am talking about the deeper things. Do people always come to you for advice? Are you the one who can make anyone laugh, no matter how shitty their day has been? Are you the one who walks into a mess and instinctively knows how to fix it?

These things matter. They are not coincidences. They are the universe tapping you on the shoulder saying, *hey, this is part of what you are here to do.*

Stop Hiding Your Magic and Start Using It

Here is where a lot of people get stuck. They recognize their gifts, but instead of owning them, they play small. They convince themselves that their talents are not *special enough* or *important enough* to be their purpose.

That is absolute bullshit.

Your gifts are meant to be used. Not just for your own fulfillment, but to impact the world around you. They were never meant to be hidden, doubted, or kept small to make others comfortable. You were given these abilities for a reason, and that reason is bigger than your fear, your self-doubt, or the voice in your head that tells you, *Who do you think you are?*

Your soul's purpose is not just about what you get out of life—it is about what you give. It is about how you show up, how you serve, and how you let your unique talents create a ripple effect of healing, inspiration, and transformation. And guess what? When you start using your gifts in a way that benefits others, everything shifts.

Life gets richer.

Your work, relationships, and everyday interactions start to feel more meaningful.

Things just *click* in a way they never did before.

But let's be real for a second. For so long, I struggled with feeling *worthy* of charging for my gifts. I convinced myself that if I was truly called to help others, I should just do it out of the kindness of my heart. I gave away my time, my energy, my skills—until I was drained, depleted, and wondering why I felt unappreciated.

Here is what I finally realized: **Honoring your worth is part of the work.**

When you refuse to charge for your gifts, when you downplay your abilities, when you shrink yourself out of fear of being judged, you are not being humble—you are *blocking* the very abundance that is meant to flow through you.

Charging for your gifts does not make you greedy. It makes you sustainable.

It allows you to keep doing what you love *without* resentment, exhaustion, or burnout. It allows you to show up at your best for the people who truly value what you bring to the table.

You were not put on this earth to scrape by, to constantly over give, or to apologize for wanting to be compensated for your time and energy. You were put here to *thrive*, to share, and to fully step into the power of who you are.

So if you have been holding back, if you have been waiting for some magical sign to give yourself permission—*this is it.*

Use your gifts. Honor your worth, stop feeling guilty for receiving in return. Because when you finally embrace your purpose *fully*, you do not just change your own life.

You change the world.

So, take a second and ask yourself:

- How can I use my gifts to make a difference?
- What lights me up *and* brings value to others?
- Where am I holding back because I am afraid to fully step into my power?

Maybe you are meant to inspire others with your art, music, or writing. Maybe your purpose is tied to healing, whether that is through energy work, coaching, or simply being the kind of person who makes others feel *seen*. Maybe you are meant to create, to innovate, to *build* something that did not exist before you decided to bring it to life.

Whatever it is, *own it*. Stop waiting for permission. Stop worrying if it is "good enough" or if other people will approve. Your gifts are not up for debate. They are not something you have to justify. They are part of what makes you *you*, and the more you embrace them, the more aligned you will feel.

Your Purpose is Not Just About You—It is About Impact

Here is the truth about purpose that most people miss. It is not just about what makes *you* happy. It is about *how you use your gifts to help others*.

I do not care how introverted, socially awkward, or anti-people you think you are. Your purpose is *always* going to involve some kind of contribution to the world. Because we are not here to live in isolation. We are here to create, to connect, to influence, to *leave things better than we found them.*

Think about the people who have impacted *your* life. The ones who inspired you, encouraged you, lifted you up when you were down. Did they change the whole world? Probably not. But they changed *your* world. And that is what purpose is about.

So, how can you start using your gifts right now? Not someday. *Today.* Maybe it is as simple as sharing your story so that someone else does not feel so alone. Maybe it is teaching, mentoring, or leading in a way that empowers others. Maybe it is turning that business idea, that book, that project you have been sitting on into something real.

The point is, *do something.* Your gifts were never meant to be hoarded. They were meant to be *shared.*

Final Thoughts: Stop Playing Small and Start Owning Your Power

If you take nothing else from this, remember this one thing—your gifts were given to you for a reason. They are not random. They are not meaningless. They are *yours* because they are part of what you are meant to contribute to this world.

Stop downplaying them. Stop telling yourself you are not talented enough, smart enough, creative enough, or *worthy enough* to use them. You are.

Start looking at the things you love doing, the things that come naturally to you, the things that make you feel *alive*, and ask yourself how you can use them to step further into your purpose. Because when you do, something shifts. Life stops feeling like a constant uphill battle and starts flowing the way it was meant to. You stop questioning if you are on the right path, because suddenly, everything starts aligning.

So go ahead. Own your magic. Use your damn gifts. The world needs what you have to offer, and the longer you hold back, the longer someone else is waiting for what *only you* can bring.

And if that is not motivation enough, then just remember—life is too damn short to keep playing small.

Step 5: Get Messy, Make Mistakes, and Try Everything

Figuring out your purpose is not some perfectly curated, effortless journey where everything magically falls into place overnight. It is an unpredictable, sometimes frustrating, sometimes exhilarating process. Your path is not a straight road neatly laid out ahead of you. It is more like a maze with detours, dead ends, unexpected shortcuts, and a few places where you swear you have been before but have no clue how you got back there.

And that is exactly how it is *supposed* to be.

The pressure to have it all figured out from day one is a myth. Nobody wakes up knowing exactly what they are meant to do in life, and if they claim they did, they are either lying or conveniently forgetting all the times they questioned everything. The truth is, discovering your purpose is a hands-on process. You must *do* things, try things, fail at things, and stumble into unexpected opportunities. It is through experimenting that you uncover what lights you up and what drains the life out of you.

Give Yourself Permission to Explore

Too many people stay stuck because they are waiting for the perfect plan before they take action. They think they need a clear vision, a foolproof strategy, and a sign from the universe that says, *this is it!* before they dare to step forward. But that is not how this works. Clarity comes *after* action, not before.

Stop overthinking. Just start.

Take that art class you have been eyeing, even if you have convinced yourself, you are not creative. Volunteer for a cause that tugs at your heart, even if you are not sure how you will fit in. Start that business, that blog, that side project that has been rattling around in your brain, even if it makes no sense on paper. Not everything you try will be *the thing*—but every single experience will teach you something about yourself.

Some of the best discoveries come from the most unexpected places. Maybe you sign up for a yoga retreat just to de-stress, and it ends up unlocking a deep passion for healing work. Maybe you start writing a blog as a creative outlet, and before you know it, people are reaching out, telling you how much your words resonate with them. Maybe you take a temporary job just to pay the bills, and it introduces you to a passion you never saw coming.

Everything you try is a stepping stone. Every new experience adds another piece to the puzzle. Even the so-called *failures* are valuable, because they help you eliminate what is *not* for you.

Step Outside of Your Comfort Zone

You cannot find your purpose if you never push yourself beyond what feels familiar. Growth does not happen inside the bubble of routine. It happens when you try something that stretches you, challenges you, and maybe even terrifies you a little.

That does not mean you have to quit your job, sell your belongings, and move to a mountaintop to find yourself. It can be as simple as saying yes to something new, even when part of you wants to run in the other direction.

Maybe you have always wanted to speak on stage but have convinced yourself you are not a "public speaker." Sign up for a local event and test it out. Maybe you love creating things but doubt that anyone would actually pay for your work. Put it out there anyway. Maybe you have spent years in a career that feels like it is suffocating you, but leaving feels impossible. Start exploring other paths, even if you are not ready to make a full leap just yet.

The point is, if you never *try*, you will never know.

And yes, it will be uncomfortable. Yes, you might feel like an imposter at first. Yes, you will have moments where you think, *What the hell am I doing?* But discomfort is not a sign to stop. It is a sign that you are growing.

Your Purpose Will Evolve, and That is a Good Thing

One of the biggest lies people believe is that they have to find *one* purpose that will define them forever. That is complete nonsense. Your purpose is not a single, unchanging destination. It shifts and expands as you grow.

Who you are today is not the same person you were five years ago, and it will not be the same person you are five years from now. The things that light you up may change. The way you express your purpose may evolve. That is *not* a sign of failure or confusion—it is a sign of growth.

Maybe what once felt like your life's mission no longer excites you, and you feel guilty for wanting something different. That is normal. Maybe you have invested years into a path that no longer aligns with who you are. That does not mean those years were wasted—it means they led you to a new chapter.

Give yourself the freedom to pivot. Allow yourself to evolve. Your purpose is not a fixed point; it is an unfolding journey.

Trust the Process, Even When It Feels Messy

There will be times when you feel lost. Times when you second-guess yourself. Times when nothing makes sense, and you wonder if you are ever going to figure it all out. Those moments are part of the process.

You do not have to have all the answers today. You just have to *keep moving*. Keep trying, keep exploring, keep putting yourself out there. Every experience—good, bad, and in-between—is shaping you, leading you, guiding you toward the life you are meant to live.

So, stop waiting for certainty, stop waiting for perfection, and stop waiting for permission. Just start. The path will reveal itself as you walk it.

Living in Alignment with Your Purpose

Once you start getting a grip on what your soul's purpose actually is, the next step is to start living in alignment with it. And no, that does not mean you need to quit your job, sell your belongings, and move to a remote jungle to "find yourself" (unless, of course, that is your jam, in which case, go live your best jungle life). What it *does* mean is making intentional choices every single day that reflect who you truly are and what actually lights you up inside.

I know this because I have been on both sides of the fence. For years, I tried to fit into spaces that never quite felt right. I worked jobs that drained me, surrounded myself with people who did not really see *me*, and lived in ways that dulled my spirit instead of fueling it. And I convinced myself that was just *life*. But deep down, I always knew I was meant for something *bigger*. That little whisper inside me never shut up, even when I tried to drown it out with distractions.

Then, life threw me some curveballs—ones that made me stop in my tracks and ask myself, *What the hell am I even doing?* I finally had to face the fact that I was not living in alignment with the person I was meant to be. So, I started making changes. Small ones at first. Saying no to things that did not feel right. Prioritizing the work that actually made me *feel* something. Allowing myself to be more of who I truly am, without worrying about who it would make uncomfortable. And let me tell you, once I started living my truth, everything started shifting. My career, my relationships, my confidence, my happiness—it all started clicking into place.

The truth is, living in alignment with your purpose does not require some grand, dramatic overhaul. It starts with the little things. Saying yes to opportunities that excite you, even if they scare you a little. Saying no to the things that drain your energy and leave you feeling like a shell of yourself. Taking up space in ways that feel *right*, instead of shrinking yourself to fit where you do not belong.

Think of it as a series of small but powerful choices that, over time, completely transform your life. Maybe it is choosing to spend your Saturday morning working on that passion project instead of mindlessly scrolling social media. Maybe it is deciding to finally put yourself out there in a way you never have before starting that blog, taking that class, pitching that idea, or just speaking your truth without filtering yourself.

And when you start living in alignment with your purpose, something amazing happens. You feel *lighter*. More grounded. More *you*. It is like stepping into a version of yourself that has always been there, just waiting for you to catch up.

Aligning Actions with Purpose

Knowing your purpose is one thing. Living it is where the magic happens. This is where you stop just talking about what you want and start *being* the person who actually *does the damn thing*.

When your actions align with your purpose, life starts feeling *intentional*. There is a deep sense of fulfillment that comes from knowing that how you spend your time, energy, and effort actually *matters*. You wake up with more clarity. You stop feeling like you are just going through the motions. Even when life throws challenges at you, they feel *different*— less like random chaos and more like part of a bigger picture.

But let's be honest, this is not always easy. Living in alignment with your purpose requires you to *choose yourself* over and over again. And that is not always comfortable. It might mean walking away from relationships that no longer fit. It might mean quitting that job that sucks the soul right out of you. It might mean stepping into a new version of yourself that some people will not understand—and that is okay.

To start aligning your actions with your purpose, ask yourself:

- Are the things I do every day supporting the life I *actually* want?
- Am I making choices based on *my* values, or am I just trying to meet expectations that are not even mine?
- Where in my life am I *out of alignment*, and what can I change to fix that?

If you feel like your daily life does not reflect who you really are, then it is time to make some adjustments. Maybe that means setting better boundaries. Maybe that means letting go of commitments that no longer serve you. Maybe that means finally taking the leap on something you have been putting off because fear has been whispering in your ear.

One of the best ways to stay aligned is through regular check-ins with yourself. Whether it is journaling, meditation, or just taking five minutes each day to ask, *Am I living in a way that feels right?* —this kind of reflection keeps you from drifting off course. And trust me, when you start paying attention, you *will* notice when something feels off.

Living Your Truth is a Process, Not a Destination

This is not a one-time thing where you suddenly "arrive" at your purpose and never have to think about it again. Life does not work like that. Your purpose will evolve as you grow. What feels aligned today might shift in a few years—and that is a *good* thing.

The key is to stay open, to keep learning, to keep following what *feels right*. Your purpose is not something you have to force. It is something that naturally unfolds when you listen to yourself, trust your instincts, and make choices that *honor* who you are.

And most importantly—do not wait for permission. Do not wait until you "feel ready." Do not waste another second doubting whether you are *worthy* of the life you actually want. You *are*. The only thing standing in the way is the version of you that still thinks they have to play small.

So, step up. Start making choices that align with your purpose. Show up as the person you were always meant to be. And watch how everything changes.

Strategies for Making Sure Your Daily Life Actually Matches Your Soul's Calling

Living in alignment with your soul's calling is not something that happens by accident. It is an intentional choice, made over and over again, in a world that constantly tries to pull you in a hundred different directions. It is easy to get caught up in the daily grind, where your purpose gets buried under deadlines, errands, and the soul-sucking vortex that is answering emails. But here is the truth—when your actions reflect your purpose, life does not just *happen* to you anymore. You become the architect, designing a life that feels meaningful, fulfilling, and, dare I say, actually enjoyable.

So, how do you make sure that your daily actions align with your higher calling? How do you keep yourself from drifting into autopilot mode where you wake up one day and realize you have spent the last five years doing things that do not even light you up? The answer lies in being *deliberate*. Below are some strategies to help you stay on track, no matter how chaotic life gets.

Start Every Day with Intention

Your day is like a blank canvas, and how you begin it sets the tone for everything that follows. If you roll out of bed, immediately check your phone, and dive into the chaos without a second thought, you are basically handing over the reins to whatever distractions the world throws at you. Instead, start your day with a moment of *deliberate intention*.

This does not have to be complicated. Maybe it is a quick journal entry, a few minutes of meditation, or simply taking a deep breath and asking yourself, *what do I want to focus on today?* The goal is to remind yourself of your purpose *before* the world has a chance to pull you off course.

Check Yourself Before You Wreck Yourself

Throughout the day, pause before making decisions—big or small—and ask, *does this align with my purpose?* Now, I am not saying you need to question whether making a sandwich is in alignment with your higher calling (although, if your purpose involves culinary artistry, then by all means, analyze that sandwich). But when it comes to how you spend your time, who you give your energy to, and which opportunities you say yes or no to, *mindful decision-making* is a game changer.

If something feels *off*, take a step back and ask why. Are you doing this because it genuinely excites you, or are you doing it out of obligation? Is this pushing you toward your true self, or is it just another distraction?

Aligning with your purpose means learning when to pivot, when to decline, and when to chase something wholeheartedly.

Build a Routine That Supports Your Purpose

If your days feel like an exhausting game of catch-up, chances are your routine is not working for you—it is working *against* you. Living with purpose requires structure, even if that structure is loose and flexible. It is about making sure that the things that *matter most* are built into your daily life.

What does that look like? It could mean scheduling time for your passion project before your energy gets drained by everything else. It might mean carving out space for spiritual practices, movement, or creative work that fuels you. Maybe it is making sure you start and end your day with activities that actually feed your soul, not just your social media addiction. The point is, if you do not intentionally create time for the things that align with your calling, they will always take a backseat to life's endless distractions.

Reflect, Adjust, Repeat

Think of your purpose like a GPS. If you are driving toward a destination and realize you have taken a wrong turn, you do not just keep going in the wrong direction and hope for the best. You *course correct*. Living in alignment with your soul's calling works the same way.

Take time each day, or at least once a week, to reflect on whether your actions are supporting your purpose. Did you spend your time in ways that felt meaningful? Or did you get sidetracked by things that do not actually matter? This is not about being hard on yourself—it is about *noticing* so you can make adjustments.

Journaling is a fantastic way to track your alignment. Writing things down helps you see patterns, recognize what is working, and catch yourself before you fall into routines that do not serve you. Over time, these reflections help you sharpen your focus and make living in alignment second nature.

Set Boundaries Like Your Life Depends on It— Because It Kind of Does

If you do not protect your time and energy, the world will happily consume every last drop of it. Aligning your actions with your purpose means learning to say *no*—a lot. No to commitments that drain you. No to people who do not respect your time. No to obligations that have nothing to do with the life you are trying to create.

Boundaries are not selfish. They are necessary. The more you say no to what does not serve you, the more space you create for what *does*.

If saying no makes you uncomfortable, start small. Practice turning down requests that feel like a waste of time. Politely decline invitations that you *know* you do not want to attend. Remove yourself from situations that constantly drain your energy. The people who genuinely support your journey will understand. The ones who get offended? Well, that just proves why they should not have access to your time in the first place.

Surround Yourself with People Who Get It

Your environment plays a massive role in whether or not you stay aligned with your purpose. If you are constantly surrounded by people who do not respect your goals, who drain your energy, or who belittle your aspirations, staying on track is going to feel like running a marathon with weights strapped to your ankles.

Find your *people*—the ones who lift you up, who challenge you to grow, and who inspire you to keep pushing forward. They do not have to be on the exact same path as you, but they should at least *respect* the journey you are on. And if you do not have those kinds of people in your immediate circle, seek them out. Join groups, attend events, connect online. You deserve to be surrounded by individuals who encourage you to *step into your power*, not shrink away from it.

Celebrate the Small Wins

Every time you make a choice that aligns with your purpose, celebrate it. Living your truth is not always easy, and every little step you take in the right direction deserves recognition. Maybe you finally said no to something that drained you. Maybe you made progress on a project that excites you. Maybe you just *felt* more like yourself today than you did yesterday.

Acknowledge it. Celebrate it. Let yourself *feel* the progress you are making, even if it is small. The more you reinforce these choices, the easier it becomes to keep making them.

Be Patient and Give Yourself Grace

Alignment is a process, not a destination. There will be days when you nail it, and days when you feel completely off track. That is okay. The key is to keep showing up, keep adjusting, and keep choosing yourself over and over again.

You are not meant to have all the answers right away. You are meant to learn, grow, evolve, and refine your path as you go. So be patient with yourself. Give yourself grace when things do not go as planned. And most importantly, trust that as long as you keep taking steps in the right direction, you *will* get where you are meant to be.

At the end of the day, this is your life, your journey, your purpose. Make it count.

A Glimpse into My Personal Journey

This is not just a story about addiction, heartbreak, and hitting rock bottom. This is about what happens when you finally stop running from yourself, when you stop drowning out the pain and start facing the truth—raw, unfiltered, and sometimes, ugly as hell.

I did not always know my purpose. Hell, for most of my life, I was too busy self-destructing to even ask the question. But looking back now, I can see how every dark moment, every wrong turn, and every painful lesson led me here. So, let's start at the beginning—the part where I did everything I could to escape who I really was.

Drinking, Running, and the Boy Who Introduced Me to Cocaine

My relationship with alcohol started young. It was my escape, my way of numbing out, my way of pretending I was not drowning in a past I did not know how to deal with. But if alcohol was my first love, then cocaine was the one that swept me off my feet and led me straight into chaos.

I had just survived a failed suicide attempt, my stomach pumped after washing down a bottle of Xanax with Yukon Jack. I was lost, empty, and looking for something—*anything*—to make me feel alive. And then I met *him*.

He was wild, charismatic, and he had a taste for partying that made my own self-destructive tendencies look like child's play. It was the mid-2000s, and before I knew it, I had dropped everything—my friends, my family, any shred of stability I had left—and moved to Seattle with him.

That was where I was introduced to cocaine. I hated it at first. The burn, the rush, the way it made my heart race. But it did something else too— it silenced the noise. It gave me a way to escape my reality, the painful truth of where I really came from.

And just like that, I was hooked.

For the next few years, we traveled all over the country, partying, living it up, convincing ourselves that this reckless, drug-fueled lifestyle was *freedom*. But the thing about running is that you always run out of road eventually. And when our relationship exploded into an ugly, violent mess, I found myself homeless, with a black eye, and no clue what the hell to do next.

So, I went back to Oregon.

New Beginnings, Old Demons

When I returned, I had nothing. No money, no home, no real plan. But sometimes, the universe sends you exactly what you need. I ended up moving in with two complete strangers—two men who would become some of my greatest friends. They gave me a fresh start, a safe place to land when I was at my lowest.

And what did I do with that fresh start? I jumped right back into exotic dancing, because at the time, it was the only world I knew. It was fast money, an easy distraction, and it kept me from having to sit still long enough to *feel* anything real.

But then I met Todd.

He was different. He was kind, stable, compassionate. The kind of man who saw *through* people, past the bullshit, straight to their soul. I tried everything to scare him off—bombarding him with my war stories, my wild past, all the reasons why I was too damaged for someone like him.

But he was not afraid. He saw something in me that I could not yet see in myself.

He was the start I needed.

He showed me what unconditional love looked like, what safety felt like. He was patient, supportive, and he *showed up* in ways no one else ever had. He loved me through my chaos, through my self-sabotage, through all the walls I put up to keep people out.

But even then—I was still running.

We got married, we had a baby, we built a life, but I was still drowning myself in cocaine, still numbing out, still avoiding the one thing I needed to face—*myself*. And because I could not sit alone with my own demons, I did what I had always done. I ran.

I left him, shattered his heart, and ran straight into the arms of a narcissistic asshole who, looking back, was exactly the kind of man I *thought* I deserved. Not someone who loved me the way he did, but someone who reflected back all the self-hatred I was carrying inside.

And that is my greatest regret. Not my addiction, not my past, not even the mistakes I made in survival mode—but the pain I caused Todd. The one person who had *seen* me, and I left because I was too busy running from myself.

Six Years of Toxicity and the Night Everything Changed

I stayed in that toxic cycle for *six years*.

Six years of fighting. Six years of being cheated on. Six years of believing that I *deserved* the misery because, deep down, I was still punishing myself for what I had done.

And then, on **New Year's Eve 2019**, in the middle of yet another fight, something inside me snapped. I looked at the vodka in my hand, looked at the man in front of me, and I finally saw it for what it was—*a cycle I was never going to escape if I did not make the choice to end it right then and there.*

So, I put the drink down.

I walked away from alcohol that night and never looked back.

Sober, but Still Choosing the Wrong Men

But sobriety was not the magic fix. I was sober, but I was still choosing men who were bad for me. The first was a sociopath, a man who took my vulnerability and my deepest traumas—the ones I had confided in him about—and used them as ammunition to break me down. He would scream at me, call me broken, make me feel like I was unworthy of love.

After him came the next lesson. Frank was kind, sweet even, and I *knew* from the very beginning he was not good for me. He was an alcoholic. But I chose him anyway. Maybe I saw his potential. Maybe I thought that if I shined my light bright enough, it would lead him out of his darkness.

It did not.

Instead, his darkness began to snuff out my light. I found myself constantly getting angry when he would come home drunk. Because I knew what that meant, it meant his day was spent doing his typical flirtatious behaviors with other women. I even looked the other way when he was caught having kissed another woman the very same day, he was moving his things into my home.

I stayed, even through the betrayal, even through the hurt, because I was afraid for his life. He was drinking himself to death, and I thought if I left, he would not survive.

But what about *me*?

I finally had to remember why I started writing these books, why I had worked so hard to reclaim my life. How could I help others if I was falling back into the same old patterns? How could I teach self-worth if I was still choosing others over myself? I felt in that moment like I was not being true to my soul's purpose again.

So as painful as it was, I ended it. He hurts, I hurt... but it was not just an act of self-love, it was also an act of love toward him. Letting go was not just about saving myself. It was about giving him the space to face his own demons without me standing in the way, without me softening the consequences, without me making excuses for him. Because that is what I had been doing. I thought I was helping, but in reality, I was enabling. I was cushioning his rock bottom, trying to love him into sobriety, trying to heal wounds that were never mine to fix.

But real love does not mean setting yourself on fire to keep someone else warm. It does not mean losing yourself in someone else's chaos just because you are afraid of what will happen if you walk away.

I had to let him go so that he could have the chance to heal. I had to let him go so *I* could continue healing. Staying would have only kept us both trapped—him in his addiction and me in a cycle I had worked so hard to break.

And that was the hardest part. Because loving someone does not always mean holding on. Sometimes, the greatest act of love is walking away and trusting that they will find their way.

He hurts. I hurt. But for the first time in a long time, I am choosing *me*. And in doing so, I am finally honoring the purpose that has been calling me all along.

The universe was not done teaching me.

It all started at the Kava bar, where our friendship was supposed to be *just that*—a friendship. But from the very beginning, there was something different, something neither of us could put into words. A pull. A connection that was instant and undeniable, like we had known each other long before this lifetime.

We both felt it.

It was not just about chemistry or attraction. It was something mystical, something that went beyond logic. A soul-level recognition, as if the universe had been slowly weaving our paths together, waiting for the exact right moment for us to collide. And when we did, there was no stopping it.

What started as a simple friendship became a love story unlike anything I have ever known. It was not a whirlwind romance built on fleeting passion. It was a force, steady and unshakable, yet deeply electric. Justin was not just someone new—he was someone who had been there all along, waiting for the right time to step forward. It is as if the universe conspired to bring us together at the exact moment, I was finally ready to *choose myself*.

This is not just love. It is one of the most powerful connections I have ever experienced. Because it is not just about us. It is about something bigger. Something meant. Something *written in the stars* long before we ever found each other again.

Justin sees me, I mean truly sees me. He reflects all the beauty I have built, the strength I have gained, and the love I have finally learned to accept. And the best part? He is sober too.

For the first time in my life, I am not running. I am standing still. I am fully present. I am finally choosing *me*. And in doing that, I have found a love that mirrors the one I have been learning to cultivate within myself all along.

Chapter 6

The Power of Connection

"True connection is the bridge between hearts, where
understanding flows, healing begins, and the soul
finds home in the presence of another." —Jamie

Alright, let's talk about connection. Not the Wi-Fi kind (although, let's be honest, losing a strong signal can send anyone into a spiral). I'm talking about the kind of connection that doesn't require a password, an app, or a desperate call to tech support. This is about the deep, human-to-human kind of connection—the kind that fuels our souls, keeps us sane, and reminds us that we're not just aimlessly floating around in this chaotic mess called life.

But let's be honest, forming real connections these days can feel like trying to navigate a minefield. Between social media distractions, packed schedules, and the general awkwardness of putting yourself out there, it can seem easier to keep interactions surface-level. It's like we're all just bumper cars at the county fair—crashing into each other with a polite smile before zooming off in our own direction. We might send the occasional "how have you been?" text or toss out a half-hearted "we should totally hang out soon," but true, meaningful connection? That takes effort. And effort takes energy, which, let's be real, most of us are already rationing like we're in the middle of the apocalypse.

Yet, no matter how independent, introverted, or "I'd rather just stay home" you might be, deep down, we *all* crave connection. We all want to feel seen, heard, and understood. We want people in our lives who celebrate our highs, hold us through our lows, and remind us that we're not alone when everything goes to shit. That's what this chapter is about—how to cultivate real, authentic connections, the kind that go beyond small talk and meaningless pleasantries. The kind that actually *matters*.

Why Connection Matters

Humans are wired for connection. Seriously, science backs it up. Our brains light up like a Christmas tree when we experience genuine moments of connection. Oxytocin, the "bonding hormone," floods our system when we share laughter, love, or even just a deep, heartfelt conversation. It's what makes us feel safe, understood, and, quite frankly, *less like a raging dumpster fire of emotions*.

Connection grounds us. It reminds us that we're not alone in our struggles. It gives us a sense of purpose, a reason to get out of bed on the days when the weight of the world feels unbearable. Ever notice how a simple conversation with the right person can make your entire day feel lighter? That's because connection has the power to heal, inspire, and breathe life into even the most exhausted, coffee-dependent souls.

And let's not forget—life is *meant* to be shared. The best moments in life become even better when they're experienced with people who truly get you. Whether it's your best friend, your partner, your chosen family, or that random stranger at the grocery store who made you laugh at the self-checkout line, connection is what makes life feel *real*.

The Different Types of Connection

Connection comes in many forms, and each serves its own purpose in our lives.

1. Soul-Level Friendships

These are your ride-or-die people. The ones who have seen you ugly cry, know your deepest fears, and will show up at your door with snacks and terrible advice when you need them most. They are the people who don't just tolerate you—they *cherish* you.

2. Romantic Connections

Love is one of the most powerful forms of connection, but let's be real, it's also one of the trickiest. We all have a history, a past that shapes how we give and receive love. The key to deep, meaningful romantic connections? Vulnerability, trust, and finding someone who reflects back the best parts of you—not just the parts you're trying to fix.

3. Family Bonds (Biological or Chosen)

Family isn't always about blood. Sometimes, the deepest connections come from the people who step in when your biological family doesn't show up the way they should. Whether it's the family you were born into or the one you built yourself, these connections shape the foundation of who you are.

4. Casual but Meaningful Encounters

Not every connection has to be lifelong to be meaningful. Sometimes, a five-minute conversation with a stranger can shift your entire perspective. A kind word, a shared moment of understanding—these seemingly small interactions can have a huge impact on our day, or even our lives.

Building Stronger Connections

So, how do you cultivate deeper, more meaningful connections? How do you move past surface-level interactions and build relationships that actually *matter*?

1. Be Present

Put down your phone. Stop scrolling. Look people in the eye. *Listen* to what they're saying instead of just waiting for your turn to speak. Presence is the foundation of every strong connection.

2. Be Vulnerable (Even When It's Uncomfortable as Hell)

Real connection requires *realness*. That means dropping the facade, letting people see who you truly are, and risking rejection for the sake of authenticity. It's scary as hell, but it's also the only way to form bonds that actually *mean* something.

3. Choose Quality Over Quantity

A handful of deep, meaningful relationships will always be more fulfilling than a thousand acquaintances who don't really know you. It's not about *how many* people you know—it's about how deeply you connect with the ones who matter.

4. Give What You Want to Receive

If you want support, be supportive. If you want deeper conversations, initiate them. If you want loyalty, be loyal. Connection is a two-way street, and the energy you put in is the energy you'll get back.

5. Let Go of One-Sided Relationships

Not every connection is meant to last. Some people will only meet you at the level of effort you're willing to give. If a relationship is consistently draining you instead of fueling you, it's okay to let it go. Connections should uplift, not exhaust.

The Magic of True Connection

At the end of the day, connection is what makes life worth living. It's the shared laughter, the deep conversations, the knowing glances across the room when words aren't even necessary. It's the people who remind you who you are when you start to forget.

And the best part? Connection is limitless. There are always new people to meet, new friendships to form, and new love to discover. The universe has a funny way of bringing the right people into your life at the right time, and when you're open to it, magic happens.

So, as we dive into this chapter, let's explore how to build, nurture, and cherish the connections that truly matter. Because at the end of the day, life is not just about what you *do*—it's about *who* you share it with.

Finding My Soul Tribe

Connection is what makes life worth living. There's something life changing about being truly seen. Not for the mask you wear, not for the roles you play but for the raw, unfiltered you. The kind of people who don't flinch at your truth, who hold space for your messy moments without trying to fix or judge them. These are your soul people, the ones who don't just walk with you through the light, but sit beside you in the dark without needing to flip it back on.

For a long time, I tried to force connections that looked good on the outside but felt hollow underneath. I stayed in friendships out of habit, out of guilt, out of the fear that I'd be alone if I let go. But your soul tribe doesn't need to be convinced to love you. They show up, not because you're perfect, but because they recognize something familiar in your fire. Finding them isn't about collecting people, it's about releasing the ones who drain you so the right ones finally have room to come in.

And sometimes, those people, the ones who truly see you, who feel like home even when you have just met, appear right when you need them most.

For me, that moment happened when I decided it was time to stop isolating myself and start finding my circle. After years of choosing relationships that drained me, friendships that felt conditional, and a life that often left me feeling like I was standing on the outside looking in, I knew something had to change. I needed to find my people, the ones who not only accepted me but truly understood me, the ones who resonated with my energy and reflected back the light I had spent so many years rediscovering.

And as fate would have it, I found them at a **Kava Bar**.

Now, if you are unfamiliar with **Kava**, it is a root that has been used for centuries in the South Pacific for its calming, stress-relieving effects. It has this beautiful way of easing anxiety, helping people transition from addiction to sobriety, and creating a space where deep, authentic conversations flow as easily as the kava itself. Unlike alcohol, kava does not numb you or make you forget—it allows you to feel present, to connect with yourself and those around you in a way that is raw, honest, and deeply grounding.

It was through my sister **Dawn** that I was introduced to **Bula Kava House**, and from the moment I walked in, I felt something shift. There was an energy in that space—a mix of warmth, acceptance, and this unspoken understanding that everyone there was on their own journey, but somehow, our paths had all converged for a reason.

And that is when I started to meet the humans who would become my soul tribe. But first let's talk about my **baby sister, Dawn**—because even though she's my sister by blood, she's also one of the deepest soul connections I've ever had. Since she moved to Oregon to be closer to me, our bond has only grown stronger, and honestly, I don't know what I'd do without her. She has been a **beacon of love and grounding energy**, pulling me from the trenches of my own despair in the times I needed her most. She doesn't just love me—she **sees** me, in all my chaos, my growth, my struggles, and my strength. And through it all, she has offered me so much healing, never wavering, never judging—just holding space for me in a way that only someone who truly loves you can.

Dawn is like **a walking embodiment of sunshine and wildflowers,** a **free-spirited, vibrant hippie soul** who reminds me every day that life is meant to be lived with an open heart. She loves with every fiber of her being, and she moves through life with this effortless grace that I truly admire. She has shown me how to embrace love without fear, how to be soft without being weak, and how to dance through the storms instead of just waiting for them to pass. Her presence in my life is a gift, and I am endlessly grateful for the way she has helped me heal just by **being who she is.**

Nyko: The Radiant Soul

The first was **Nyko**, my sister's roommate and one of the kindest, most radiant souls I have ever encountered. He is the type of person who carries light wherever he goes—his energy is magnetic, his laughter contagious, and his heart so open that you can *feel* it just being in his presence. He sees the beauty in the world, in people, in the small, everyday moments most overlook. His soul shines so brightly, it is like he is in constant conversation with the universe, and honestly, I am convinced the universe responds.

Mossy: The Wild and Fierce Warrior

Then there is **Mossy**, a powerhouse of a woman. She is bold, unapologetic, and fierce in the way only a true warrior can be. A badass Native woman with a spirit so free it makes you want to dance barefoot in the rain and scream at the moon just to remind yourself that you are *alive*. She has this way of pushing you to step into your own power, of reminding you that you are more than your past, more than your pain—you are limitless. Being around her makes you believe in yourself in a way you might have forgotten was possible.

And then... Justin (My beautiful Scorpio Moon Man)

From the moment I saw him, I felt something shift in the air, like the universe itself paused for a moment to acknowledge that we had crossed paths once again. There was an energy between us, a familiarity that I could not explain, like we had known each other before. Not just in this life, but in every life before this one.

It was not just attraction, though there was plenty of that. It was recognition.

We both carry that heavy Scorpio energy, the kind that pulls people in, the kind that feels like intensity wrapped in mystery, the kind that is equal parts fire and water, passion and depth. It was in the way our conversations flowed effortlessly, in the unspoken understanding that sat between us like an old secret we had both forgotten but never truly lost.

With Justin, it was never about possession, never about trying to force something into a specific shape. It was about mirroring. He reflected to me all the things I had learned to love about myself, all the strength I had built, all the growth I had fought for. He saw me, not just the surface version of me, not just the parts I chose to show the world, but all of me.

And in that, I realized something.

Every single connection I had made—Nyko, Mossy, Justin—was a piece of the puzzle. They were not just people I met by chance. They were sent to me. They were part of the journey, part of my healing, part of the story that is still unfolding.

For so long, I had been searching for my place in the world, for people who felt like home. And now, here they were.

My soul tribe.

The Evolution of My Story

Meeting these souls did not just remind me of who I am, it reminded me of who I have always been. They helped me see my worth in a way that I never had before. They showed me what true, unconditional connection looks like.

Through them, I am continuing to evolve.

Through them, I am learning that love, in all its forms, is not about attachment or expectation. It is about energy. It is about resonance. It is about finding the ones who speak your language, even when no words are spoken.

Through them, I am realizing that my story is still being written.

And for the first time, I am not afraid of what comes next. Because with them beside me, I know I am exactly where I am meant to be.

Building Meaningful Relationships

Building meaningful relationships is a little like cooking the perfect meal. You need the right ingredients—trust, vulnerability, and a solid dose of authenticity. But even with the best recipe, you are going to need patience, trial and error, and maybe even a few burnt edges before you get it just right. The good news? You do not need a degree in psychology or some fancy social skills playbook to make it happen. All you need is a willingness to show up as your true self, let people in, and be present in the connections you create.

And yet, for something so essential to our happiness and well-being, relationships can feel ridiculously complicated. Maybe it is because we overthink them, or maybe it is because the world has trained us to keep our guard up, afraid of rejection, judgment, or—worst of all—being seen for exactly who we are. But here is the deal: if you want deep, fulfilling relationships, you have to be willing to get a little uncomfortable. So, let's break it down and get into the real, raw, and sometimes messy business of forming genuine connections.

Authenticity: Dropping the Mask and Showing Up as You

Let's start with authenticity—the real, unfiltered, take-it-or-leave-it version of you. This is what separates deep, lasting relationships from those surface-level, "let's talk about the weather and pretend we care" connections. Too many people walk through life putting on a front, playing roles they think others want to see. And sure, you might impress some people with your carefully curated version of yourself, but here is the catch—those people are not actually connecting with *you*. They are connecting with whatever version you are performing. And keeping that act up? It is exhausting.

So, let's make things easy. Drop the mask. Let people see you—the real you. Your quirks, your weird sense of humor, your passionate rants about things you love. The people who are meant for you, the ones who will add real value to your life, will not just accept you for who you are; they will *love* you for it. The ones who don't? Well, they were never meant to be in your corner anyway.

Authenticity creates trust, and trust is the foundation of any meaningful relationship. When you show up as yourself, you give others permission to do the same. That is where real connection begins.

Vulnerability: The Bridge Between Surface and Soul

Let's be real, vulnerability is terrifying. It is the emotional equivalent of standing on stage naked, hoping the audience claps instead of laughs.

But here's the truth: without vulnerability, relationships stay shallow. If you only ever share the polished, highlight-reel version of yourself, you never give people the chance to truly know you.

Now, I am not saying you should trauma-dump your life story on the first person who smiles at you, but being open and honest about who you are, what you feel, and what you need? That is how trust is built.

Vulnerability is not just about sharing your struggles; it is also about allowing yourself to express joy, excitement, and love without fear of looking foolish. It is about breaking down the walls that keep people at arm's length and allowing them to stand beside you instead.

Yes, it is risky. Yes, not everyone will handle it with care. But the people who do? Those are the ones worth keeping around.

Mutual Respect and Support: The Glue That Holds It All Together

Let's not forget the most crucial piece—mutual respect. Relationships are a two-way street. If one person is always the giver while the other just takes, that is not a connection, that is an energy drain. The best relationships, whether friendships, romantic partnerships, or family bonds, are built on reciprocity.

This means:

- Showing up for each other—not just when it is convenient, but when it matters.
- Listening, *really* listening, instead of just waiting for your turn to talk.
- Celebrating each other's wins without jealousy or comparison.
- Giving each other space to grow without trying to control or "fix" them.

When you invest in the people who invest in you, when you choose relationships that are built on equal give-and-take, you create a support system that lifts you up instead of weighing you down.

Fostering Meaningful Connections in Your Life

So, how do you actually build these deep, lasting relationships? Here are a few practical ways to make it happen:

- **Be intentional.** Do not just surround yourself with people out of convenience—choose relationships that bring real value to your life.
- **Make time.** Quality relationships require effort. Check in, make plans, and be present when you are with the people who matter.
- **Communicate honestly.** Speak your truth but also be willing to listen to others.
- **Let go of one-sided relationships.** If someone is not putting in effort, stop bending over backward to keep them in your life.
- **Practice gratitude.** Appreciate the people who show up for you and let them know they are valued.

Building meaningful relationships is not about finding the right people—it is about being the kind of person who attracts deep, authentic connections. It is about showing up fully, embracing who you are, and allowing others to do the same.

And who knows? Along the way, you just might find the kind of relationships that make life richer, deeper, and a hell of a lot more fun.

Embrace Your Imperfections

One of the biggest roadblocks to forming real, lasting relationships is the fear of being imperfect. So many of us fall into the trap of trying to curate the best version of ourselves, thinking that if we just seem a little more put together, a little less messy, maybe we will be more likable, more lovable, more *worthy*. But let's be honest—nobody has their shit together all the time. Nobody.

And yet, we compare ourselves to the highlight reels of others. We see the friend whose life looks so polished and effortless, like they were born inside an Instagram filter. We watch the colleague who always has the right words, the right outfit, the right amount of confidence, making it all seem so *easy*. And in doing so, we convince ourselves that we are the ones who are somehow flawed.

I have done it too. Hell, I have spent years of my life trying to outrun my imperfections. I tried to reinvent myself over and over again, thinking that if I could just create a *better* version of me, maybe I would finally be enough. When I was deep in addiction, I would mask my pain with a party-girl persona, acting like I was carefree and wild when in reality, I was drowning in self-loathing. Later, even in sobriety, I found myself choosing relationships that kept me in cycles of proving my worth. I stayed in toxic situations where I was constantly trying to fix people, to love them enough that maybe, just maybe, they would change.

And then, when I finally walked away from that last toxic relationship, I had to face something that scared the hell out of me—*myself*. Without the distractions of addiction, of chaos, of trying to fix someone else's brokenness, I was left with just *me*. And let me tell you, that was the hardest damn thing I had ever done.

But that is where the real healing began.

I had to learn to sit with myself, flaws and all, and accept that I was never *too much* or *not enough*—I was simply *me*. And that was more than enough. I had to learn that the people who truly belong in my life are the ones who see me in all my messy, complicated, imperfect glory and love me not despite of it, but *because* of it.

When I met **Justin**, something inside me shifted. He did not just see my strength—he saw my softness. He saw the scars, the past, the parts of me that I once thought made me unlovable, and he held them with care, never making me feel like I had to hide or apologize for them. And in that, I realized something I wish I had known years ago: *The right people will never ask you to shrink yourself to fit inside their world.*

True connection happens in the raw, unpolished moments. It happens when you can admit that you do not have all the answers, when you can laugh at your own mistakes, when you can cry without feeling like you are weak. It happens when you finally stop pretending to be *fine* all the damn time and allow yourself to be seen—fully, completely, and unapologetically.

And you know what happens when you do that? You give others permission to do the same. You create space for honesty, for vulnerability, for deep, meaningful relationships that are not built on the illusion of perfection but on the beauty of *realness.*

So, if you are still walking through life thinking you need to present the most polished, flawless version of yourself to be worthy of love and connection, let this be your wake-up call. Stop filtering yourself. Stop pretending to have it all together. Your imperfections are not just *acceptable*—they are the most magnetic thing about you.

The next time you feel the urge to hide the messy, unfiltered parts of yourself, remember this: *Perfection is not the goal—connection is.* And connection thrives in the real, the raw, and the wonderfully imperfect moments that make us human. So, own your quirks, embrace your flaws, and stop worrying about being someone else's definition of perfect. The right people will love you *as you are and* trust me—that is the only kind of love worth having.

Communication: The Lifeline of Connection

If authenticity is the foundation of meaningful relationships, then communication is the lifeline that keeps them alive and thriving. But let's get one thing straight. Communication is not just about talking. It is about listening. Not the kind of listening where you are just waiting for your turn to speak but really listening. It is about hearing what the other person is saying and sometimes, more importantly, what they are not saying.

Good communication means putting down your phone, turning off distractions, and actually being present. It means tuning into the tone of someone's voice, the tension in their body language, and the pauses between their words. It is not just about responding. It is about understanding. Sometimes, it is about asking the right questions to dig deeper. Other times, it is about shutting up and offering silent support. And let's be real. Sometimes it is about throwing in a well-timed joke to lighten the mood before things spiral into unnecessary drama.

Difficult conversations are uncomfortable, but they are necessary. Addressing conflict, sharing something that has been weighing on you, or setting boundaries is what takes relationships from surface level to soul deep. The key is to approach them with honesty, kindness, and just a touch of humor when appropriate. Because if we are being honest, a little well-placed sarcasm can go a long way in diffusing tension.

Learning to Communicate Without Blowing Everything Up

When I first started working with my therapist Fred, I had no idea how much my communication style resembled a wrecking ball. Subtlety was not in my vocabulary. I was either stuffing everything down until I exploded, or I was coming in hot with zero filter, full force, and emotions flying. If someone pissed me off, they knew it. If I was hurt, my response was often defensive, sharp, and let's just say, not constructive.

Fred introduced me to **Nonviolent Communication** and let me tell you, it was like discovering that I did not actually have to set things on fire just to get my point across. Turns out, you can express your needs without steamrolling people or launching into attack mode. Who knew?

At first, I thought it was just some fluffy therapist nonsense, but as I started practicing it, I realized that Nonviolent Communication was basically a cheat code for adulting in relationships. It gave me the tools to actually communicate my feelings without turning every discussion into a battle.

Let's break it down using something as simple and universally frustrating as **someone constantly leaving their socks on the floor**.

Step One: Observations Over Accusations

Instead of storming in with **"You never pick up your damn socks!"** which is basically an invitation for a fight, Nonviolent Communication suggests making a neutral observation.

"I noticed the socks are on the floor again."

No blame, no passive-aggressive tone, just stating the facts. It sets the stage for a conversation, not a confrontation.

Step Two: Expressing Feelings, Not Blame

Instead of launching into an attack, you own your emotions.

"I feel frustrated when I see socks lying around."

It is not **"You make me so angry!"** because nobody makes you feel anything. Your emotions are yours and stating them this way keeps the other person from immediately getting defensive.

Step Three: Identifying Your Needs

This is the real magic. Getting to the root of why something bothers you. Because spoiler alert. It is not just about the socks. It is about the need for respect, order, or feeling considered in your own space.

"I need a bit more order in our living space."

No attack. Just honesty.

Step Four: Making a Request, not a Demand

And finally, instead of barking orders like a drill sergeant.

"Would you be willing to put your socks in the hamper?"

Simple, direct, and most importantly, it invites cooperation instead of resistance. Nobody likes to be told what to do, but most people do not mind being asked.

Why This Actually Works

Does this mean every single request will be met with immediate compliance? No. People are still people, and some habits die hard. But what it does do is shift the conversation from blame to understanding, from defensiveness to problem-solving. It turns communication into something that strengthens relationships instead of chipping away at them.

I have used these techniques in every kind of relationship. Romantic, friendships, business partnerships. They helped me stop arguing for my pain and start advocating for my needs. They helped me set boundaries without feeling like a villain. They helped me express myself without setting things on fire.

And let's not forget. The goal is not just better communication, it is connection. Nonviolent Communication helps create an environment where both people feel heard, respected, and valued. When that happens, even the dumbest arguments, like socks on the floor, stop feeling like the end of the world and real, meaningful conversations take their place.

So, if you are out here blowing up relationships over petty shit, or on the flip side, swallowing your feelings until they fester into resentment, take a page from Fred's playbook. Speak your truth but do it in a way that invites people in instead of pushing them away. Because at the end of the day, good communication is not just about making your point. It is about making your relationships stronger.

Invest in Quality Time

Time is one of those things we all claim we never have enough of, but somehow, we manage to binge-watch an entire season of a show in one weekend. The truth is time is not something you *find*—it is something you *make* for the people and things that actually matter. And when it comes to relationships, if you are not putting in the time, you are not building the connection. It is that simple.

Meaningful relationships do not magically appear because you send a few texts or drop the occasional meme in someone's DMs. They require effort, intention, and a willingness to prioritize the people who bring value to your life. Think of it like maintaining a garden. If you only water it when you feel like it, eventually, everything wilts, and you are left wondering why your friendships or relationships feel like they are dying.

Now, this does not mean you need to schedule some elaborate bonding experience every other day. Who has time for that? Not me, and probably not you either. But small, consistent efforts? That is where the magic happens. A quick check-in, a spontaneous call, or even a simple "thinking about you" text can go a long way in making people feel seen and valued. It is not about how *much* time you spend together, but how *intentional* you are with the time you do have.

And let's talk about presence for a second. We live in a world where everyone is juggling five things at once, and most people cannot hold a conversation without checking their phone every thirty seconds. Being *fully* present when you are with someone is an underrated superpower. Put the damn phone down, stop mentally composing your grocery list, and actually engage with the person in front of you. Look them in the eye, listen to what they are saying, and give them your full attention. Nothing says "I care about you" quite like making someone feel like they are the most important person in the room.

Quality time is about showing up, whether it is for a deep conversation, a shared laugh, or just a comfortable silence where no words are needed. It is about making people feel like they *matter*—because when you invest in relationships, they pay you back tenfold. So, stop making excuses, stop saying you will "catch up soon," and actually make the damn time. Because when it comes down to it, the relationships you nurture are the ones that will add the most richness to your life.

Practice Gratitude and Appreciation

If you want to strengthen your relationships, start with two simple words: *thank you*.

Gratitude is one of those things that seems obvious, yet we often forget to express it. We get so used to having people in our lives that we take their kindness, support, and presence for granted. But let me tell you, nothing makes someone feel undervalued faster than being treated like their efforts are expected rather than appreciated.

Showing appreciation does not mean you have to write a dramatic love letter every time someone does something nice for you. It is the small, everyday moments of acknowledgment that make the biggest impact. A simple *thank you for always being there* or *I appreciate you* can go a long way in making someone feel valued.

And let's be real, gratitude is not just good for them—it is good for *you* too. When you start focusing on what people bring into your life instead of what they lack, your entire perspective shifts. You stop nitpicking the small annoyances and start seeing the bigger picture. You realize that your best friend remembering your weird coffee order or your partner taking the trash out *without* being asked is actually a love language in itself.

Gratitude has a ripple effect. When you make a habit of expressing appreciation, the energy of that positivity spreads. People who feel valued are more likely to show up, to reciprocate, and to pour back into the relationship. It creates a cycle where connection thrives instead of withering under neglect.

So, start noticing the little things. Say *thank you* more. Let people know they matter, not just when they do something huge, but for the everyday moments that make life better. Because when people feel appreciated, they stay. And when you surround yourself with people who make life brighter, why wouldn't you want to make sure they know just how much they mean to you?

At the end of the day, relationships are not built on grand gestures. They are built on consistency, appreciation, and the effort you put in every single day. So, if you want deeper connections, stop waiting for the "perfect moment" to show up for the people in your life. The perfect moment is *right now*.

The Beauty of Connection

Building meaningful relationships is a journey—sometimes smooth, sometimes messy, and always evolving. It takes patience, effort, and a willingness to be both vulnerable and supportive. There will be misunderstandings, life will get in the way, and sometimes people will let you down. But the reward? A sense of belonging, love, and understanding that makes all the effort worthwhile.

Real connection is not about having perfect relationships. It is about having *real* ones. It is about showing up even when it is inconvenient, staying when things get messy, and embracing the beautiful chaos that comes with truly knowing and being known by another person. It is not about finding people who never make mistakes. It is about finding the ones who are willing to work through them with you.

So let yourself be seen, flaws and all. Open up those lines of communication. Make time for the people who bring joy to your life, even when it feels like there is not enough time to go around. Be the friend, the partner, the family member who listens, who shows up, who appreciates the little moments just as much as the big ones.

Because in the end, it is not the number of people in your life that matters. It is the depth of the connections you cultivate. It is about creating a network of relationships that can weather any storm, that uplift you when you are struggling, and that celebrate your victories as if they were their own. It is these meaningful connections that make life richer, more fulfilling, and truly worth living.

The Role of Authentic Relationships in the Journey of the Soul

Authentic relationships are not just about companionship or filling space in our lives. They are the mirrors that reflect our deepest truths, our most vulnerable wounds, and our greatest potential for growth. They are the catalysts that push us toward healing, self-discovery, and transformation in ways we could never achieve alone. When we strip away the superficial, the expectations, and the masks, we find that real connection is a sacred space—one where two souls meet not just to coexist, but to truly *see* and *elevate* one another.

I have learned the power of these connections firsthand. For years, I hid behind my own walls, entangled in relationships that were more about survival than soul growth. I clung to people who reflected my wounds rather than my worth, mistaking familiarity for love. I poured myself into others, trying to fix, heal, or rescue, believing that if I just loved *hard enough*, I could bring them into the light. But what I failed to see was that in doing so, I was dimming my own.

Authentic relationships are not about losing yourself in someone else. They are about finding yourself through the connection. They challenge you, break you open, and force you to confront the parts of yourself you would rather avoid. They make you uncomfortable in all the best ways because they hold up a mirror and say, *Look. Look at who you are. Look at who you are meant to be.*

When we allow ourselves to engage in relationships with honesty, openness, and vulnerability, something shifts. We create a space where real healing can take place, where we are not performing for acceptance but instead standing fully in our truth. And in this space, growth is inevitable. These connections strip away our illusions, revealing the raw, unpolished, and utterly beautiful essence of who we are.

Authentic relationships also provide the support and encouragement we need to step into our soul's purpose. When we surround ourselves with people who *see* us—not just for who we are today, but for who we are becoming—we feel safer taking risks, shedding old identities, and stepping into new, uncharted territory. These are the people who hold us up when we are too weary to hold ourselves, who remind us of our worth when we forget, who celebrate our victories as if they were their own.

On a spiritual level, these relationships remind us that we are never truly alone. They help us see beyond our individual struggles and recognize the deep interconnectedness of all souls. They teach us that love is not just something to seek—it is something to *give*. Every meaningful interaction becomes an opportunity to offer understanding, kindness, and wisdom. And in return, we receive the same.

This is why authentic relationships are not just important for personal growth. They are essential for the evolution of the soul. They remind us that our journey is not meant to be walked alone and that every person who crosses our path brings a lesson, a message, or a gift—sometimes wrapped in challenge, sometimes in love, but always with purpose.

So, seek out the relationships that push you toward expansion. Let go of the ones that keep you small. Stand in your truth, speak from your soul, and trust that the right people will hear you, see you, and walk alongside you on this journey of becoming. Because in the end, it is not just about who *we* are becoming—but about how we help each other get there.

Healing Through Connection

Healing through connection is one of the most powerful, gut-punching, life-altering experiences we can have on this wild journey of self-discovery. Let's be real, healing alone is hard as hell. Sitting in your own head, overanalyzing every past mistake, trauma, or heartbreak can feel like trying to escape quicksand. The more you fight it alone, the deeper you sink. But when you reach out, when you find your people, when you allow yourself to be *seen*, that is where the real magic happens.

We are not meant to do this healing thing solo. Sure, you can meditate in solitude, journal your heart out, or binge-watch self-help videos until your eyeballs dry up, but true transformation happens in the presence of others. It happens in those late-night conversations where you spill your guts and someone actually *listens*. It happens when a friend looks you in the eye and says, *I've been there too*, and suddenly, your burden feels a little lighter. It happens when you stop pretending you have it all together and let someone see the messy, unfiltered, beautifully flawed version of you.

When we open up and share our pain, we shatter the illusion that we are suffering alone. We realize that no one is walking through life unscathed, that everyone is carrying something heavy. And in that shared understanding, we find a kind of strength we didn't know we had. It is in that moment, when we are seen, heard, and understood, that the healing begins.

But connection is not just about comfort, it is a mirror. The people we let into our lives reflect back our wounds, our fears, our patterns. Sometimes, it is gentle, like a soft nudge, a kind word that helps us see ourselves in a new light. Other times, it is a damn bulldozer, forcing us to confront the shit we have been avoiding. That is the beauty of connection, it does not let you hide. It calls you out, holds you accountable, and challenges you to grow.

And let's talk about how healing is a two-way street. You are not just here to receive wisdom and support; you are also here to give it. Every time you share your story, every time you hold space for someone else, you are contributing to this endless cycle of healing. You never know who needs to hear *exactly* what you have been through to help them take their next step forward. That is why connection is so damn powerful. It reminds us that we are not just healing *for* ourselves, but *with* each other.

So here is the truth. Healing is not linear, and it is sure as hell not easy. There will be days when you feel like you are making progress and others where you feel like you are right back at square one. But if you have the right people around you, people who will hold space for you, remind you of your worth, and challenge you to keep going, you will get through it.

At the end of the day, connection is not just about feeling better in the moment. It is about building a foundation of trust, love, and understanding that allows us to keep moving forward, even when life knocks us flat on our asses. So, stop pretending you have to do this alone. Let people in. Find your soul tribe. Be real, be messy, be vulnerable. Because healing is not about perfection, it is about connection. And when you embrace that? That is when the real transformation begins.

Exercises

Relationship Inventory

Time for a little relationship reality check. Grab a notebook and list your five closest relationships. Now, really think about what makes these connections meaningful. Is it shared values, emotional support, or just the fact that they know exactly how you take your coffee without asking?

Next, take an honest look at where these relationships could use some TLC. Are you holding back? Are they? What's missing? How can you show up more fully and, more importantly, how can you make sure your needs are actually being met? Relationships are a two-way street, so if you find yourself doing all the work or constantly walking on eggshells, it might be time to reevaluate how much energy you're pouring into the wrong cups.

Active Listening Practice

Pick one person in your life—a partner, a friend, a coworker, even your neighbor with the strong opinions about lawn care. The next time you talk to them, try something revolutionary: *actually listen.* No mentally drafting your response while they're still talking. No zoning out and pretending to care while scrolling on your phone. Just listen, really take in their words, their emotions, their body language.

See how this changes the dynamic. When you're fully present, people notice. And when people feel heard, they open up more. It's one of the simplest yet most powerful ways to strengthen a connection—and it costs absolutely nothing but your attention.

Vulnerability Sharing

Alright, time to get a little uncomfortable. Pick a close friend or family member and share something you've been hesitant to talk about. Maybe it's a dream you've been too afraid to say out loud, a past mistake that still lingers, or a fear that's been gnawing at you. Vulnerability is where true connection happens.

Watch what happens when you open that door—does your relationship deepen? Do you feel a sense of relief? Is it easier to be yourself around them now that you're not carrying that weight alone? Vulnerability is a muscle, and the more you flex it, the stronger your connections become.

Expressing Gratitude

Nothing strengthens a relationship faster than appreciation. Write a letter to someone who has made an impact on your life. Be specific. Tell them exactly what they did that meant so much to you and how it shaped you. If you're feeling bold, read it to them in person.

This exercise isn't just for their benefit—it's for yours too. Practicing gratitude shifts your focus from what's missing to what's already incredible in your life. And trust me, when you start seeing your relationships through that lens, they become even more fulfilling.

Journal Prompts

Reflecting on Connection

- Which relationships in my life bring me the most joy and fulfillment? What makes them so strong?
- Where am I struggling in my relationships, and what's causing that tension?
- Are there any relationships that feel one-sided? Am I the one overextending, or am I the one holding back?

Exploring Vulnerability

- In what ways do I hesitate to be fully open in my relationships? What am I afraid will happen if I let my guard down?
- How can I create a space where both myself and others feel safe to be vulnerable?

Setting Intentions for Deeper Connections

- What kind of connections do I want to cultivate in my life? What steps can I take to attract those relationships?
- How can I be more intentional in the relationships I already have?

Boundaries and Balance

- Do I tend to over-give or hold back in my relationships? Where do I need to set clearer boundaries?
- Are there relationships in my life that drain me more than they fulfill me? What can I do about that?

By working through these exercises and prompts, you'll gain a deeper understanding of your relationships—where they shine, where they need work, and where you might need to make some hard choices.

The Beauty of Connection

Let's be real, relationships are messy, unpredictable, and at times, downright exhausting. But at the end of the day, they are the very thing that makes life meaningful. It's the late-night talks that heal old wounds, the inside jokes that remind you someone truly gets you, the unconditional love that carries you through your darkest days.

Meaningful relationships are not about perfection. They're about showing up—flaws, awkward moments, emotional baggage and all. They're about choosing to be present, to invest time and energy, and to nurture the connections that feed your soul.

As you move forward, remember that connection is not just about what you give, but also about what you allow yourself to receive. Be open to love, support, and genuine connection. Let yourself be seen, let yourself be heard, and most importantly, let yourself be loved.

Because at the end of the day, the relationships we build are what make this journey worth it. So cherish the good ones, put in the effort where it counts, and for the love of all things sacred, *stop wasting time on people who do not see your worth.* You deserve the kind of connections that light up your life, not the ones that drain the hell out of you.

Now, go out there and make some damn magic with the people who matter.

Chapter 7

Living with Gratitude and Abundance

"Gratitude opens the door to abundance. When we choose to see the blessings around us, life becomes a series of small miracles waiting to be celebrated."
—Jamie

Alright, welcome to the chapter where we get real about gratitude and abundance. And no, this isn't going to be one of those feel-good, "just write down three things you're grateful for" lectures. Gratitude is more than just a checklist—it's a full-blown mindset shift that has the power to flip your life from "Why does everything suck?" to "Damn, life is actually pretty amazing."

And abundance? It's not just about fat bank accounts and luxury vacations (although, let's be honest, we wouldn't say no to that). True abundance is waking up every day with the belief that you have *enough*—enough love, enough joy, enough opportunities, enough of *everything* that truly matters. And trust me, that mindset is a game-changer.

When I first started practicing gratitude, I thought it was all about forcing myself to be thankful for things I wasn't really feeling grateful for. Like, "Oh wow, I'm so grateful that my car broke down in the middle of rush hour. What a *blessing*." But the more I practiced, the more I realized that gratitude isn't about ignoring the hard stuff. It's about choosing to see the goodness *even when* the hard stuff is happening. It's not about pretending everything is perfect—it's about finding something to hold onto even when life is being a complete pain in the ass.

And let's get one thing straight—gratitude and abundance aren't things you have to *earn*. They're not exclusive to people who have it all figured out. They're available to *you*, right here, right now, exactly as you are. The key is learning how to tap into them, and that's exactly what we're about to do.

The Truth About Gratitude: It's a Superpower, not a Trend

A lot of people treat gratitude like it's some fluffy self-help trend but let me tell you—gratitude is a *badass* tool for rewiring your brain. Science even backs it up. Practicing gratitude regularly can reduce stress, improve your mood, and even help you sleep better. And I don't know about you, but I'll take all the stress relief and good sleep I can get.

When you start *actively* looking for things to be grateful for, your brain starts to rewire itself. Instead of defaulting to "What's wrong?" mode, it starts noticing what's *right*. That doesn't mean you won't have bad days. It just means that even on those bad days, you'll have a little more resilience, a little more peace, and a little less of that "everything is falling apart" feeling.

The best part? Gratitude costs *nothing*. You don't have to wait for some perfect moment to start feeling grateful—you can start right now. Look around. What's good? What's bringing you joy in this exact moment? Maybe it's your favorite song playing in the background. Maybe it's the fact that you woke up today. Maybe it's just that first sip of coffee that tastes like liquid gold. *Boom. Gratitude.*

The Myth of Scarcity: Why You Already Have More Than Enough

Let's talk about abundance, because society has done a real number on us when it comes to making us feel like we *never* have enough. Not rich enough. Not successful enough. Not pretty enough. Not loved enough. It's all BS. The whole "never enough" mindset keeps us stuck in a cycle of constantly chasing the next thing—thinking that *then* we'll finally feel fulfilled. Spoiler alert: you won't.

Abundance starts when you stop looking at what's missing and start appreciating what's already there. Instead of focusing on what you *lack*, start noticing the *overflow* in your life. The love that surrounds you. The laughter that fills your day. The random moments of beauty that show up when you least expect them. The simple pleasure of petting a dog or watching the sunset. That's abundance, and you already have more of it than you realize.

Here's the secret: when you *believe* you have enough, you actually start attracting *more*. It's not some mystical law of attraction thing—it's just that when you shift your focus to abundance, you start making choices from a place of confidence rather than fear. You take more risks, you welcome more opportunities, and you stop self-sabotaging because you *know* you're worthy of good things.

How to Cultivate Gratitude and Abundance in Your Daily Life

Alright, now that we've covered the mindset shift, let's talk about how to actually live it out. Here are some simple but powerful ways to start bringing more gratitude and abundance into your daily routine:

1. Start Your Day with a Gratitude Check

Before you even get out of bed, take a second to acknowledge *one* thing you're grateful for. Doesn't have to be deep—could be as simple as "I'm

grateful I didn't wake up to my neighbor's dog barking at 5 a.m."
Training your brain to focus on gratitude first thing in the morning sets
the tone for the rest of the day.

2. Flip the Script on Negative Thoughts

The next time you catch yourself spiraling into a negative thought pattern,
stop and ask yourself: *Is there anything good in this situation?* Even if it's
something tiny, acknowledge it. This doesn't mean ignoring your
struggles—it just means refusing to let them *consume* you.

3. Keep a "Holy Shit, My Life is Amazing" List

Forget basic gratitude lists. Start keeping a running list of all the little
moments that make you smile, laugh, or feel good. Call it whatever you
want—the point is to remind yourself that life is *full* of amazing
moments, even if some days you have to dig a little deeper to find them.

4. Give Freely Without Expecting Anything in Return

You want to bring more abundance into your life? Start *giving*. Not just
money—your time, your kindness, your support. Help someone without
expecting anything back. Compliment a stranger. Buy coffee for the
person behind you in line. The more you *give*, the more you start to
realize how much you actually *have*.

5. Celebrate Small Wins Like They're Big Deals

Stop waiting for major milestones to feel proud of yourself. Got out of
bed on a day when you felt like staying under the covers? Celebrate that.
Checked something off your to-do list? Hell yes. Every little win
matters, and when you acknowledge them, life starts to feel a lot more
abundant.

Gratitude and Abundance Are Already Yours

Here's the bottom line: gratitude and abundance aren't things you need to *chase*. They're things you *choose*. Right now. Today. In this exact moment. You don't need to wait until your life is perfect. You don't need to have all the answers. You don't need to be *more* of anything.

Start where you are. Look for the good. Recognize the abundance that already exists in your life. And watch as more and more of it flows your way.

Because life isn't about waiting for *more*. It's about *seeing* what's already right in front of you—and realizing that it's been enough all along.

1. Start Your Day with Gratitude

Instead of diving straight into the chaos of the morning, emails, social media, or whatever else is clamoring for your attention, take a few moments to reflect on what you're grateful for. Before your feet even touch the floor, pause and appreciate the small things that often go unnoticed. It could be something as simple as the warmth of your bed cocooning you in comfort, the sound of birds chirping outside your window as they welcome the new day, or even the fact that your trusty coffee maker is still holding strong, ready to deliver that first glorious cup of caffeine.

Starting your day with gratitude sets a positive tone that can carry you through even the most hectic of schedules. It's like planting seeds of positivity before the day has a chance to throw its curveballs at you. By taking just a few moments to focus on what's good, you're not only boosting your own mood but also setting yourself up to navigate the day's challenges with a little more grace and a lot less stress.

Gratitude has a way of grounding you in the present moment, reminding you that no matter how busy or chaotic life gets, there's always something to appreciate. And the beauty of it? It doesn't take much time or effort, just a conscious decision to start your day with a mindset of appreciation. So, the next time you wake up, before reaching for your phone or getting swept up in the morning rush, take a deep breath and think of something you're thankful for. It's a small habit that can make a big difference in how your day unfolds.

2. Practice the Art of 'Thank You'

We say "thank you" all the time, sometimes it's almost automatic, like a reflex. But how often do we really mean it? How often do we pause to truly feel the gratitude behind those words? The next time you express thanks, try to be more mindful about it. Look the person in the eye, offer a sincere smile, and let yourself really feel the appreciation as you say the words.

Whether it's thanking the barista who made your latte just right, the friend who listened when you needed to vent, or the coworker who stepped in to help you meet a deadline, these moments of genuine thanks have a special power. They can deepen your connections with others, making those small interactions more meaningful. Plus, when you take the time to truly acknowledge the good things people do for you, it reinforces your own sense of abundance and positivity.

Gratitude isn't just about saying the words, it's about the intention behind them. It's about recognizing the kindness, effort, and generosity of others, and letting them know that it doesn't go unnoticed. So, the next time you say, "thank you," make it count. Let it be a moment of real connection, where both you and the other person feel a little bit brighter, a little bit more appreciated, and a little bit more connected.

3. Gratitude Journaling

I know, I know—everyone talks about journaling like it's the cure for everything but hear me out. Keeping a gratitude journal doesn't have to be an elaborate process. There's no need for fancy notebooks or hours of deep reflection (unless that's your jam, in which case, go for it!). Simply jotting down three things you're thankful for each day can work wonders in shifting your focus from what's lacking to what's abundant in your life.

And let's face it, some days you might be grateful for something as basic as not spilling coffee on your shirt during a hectic morning. That's perfectly okay! Gratitude doesn't have to be profound; it just has to be genuine. What matters is that you're training your brain to notice the good, to find those little sparks of joy in the everyday moments.

Over time, this simple practice can create a ripple effect, helping you to cultivate a more positive outlook and a deeper appreciation for the life you're living—coffee stains and all. So, whether you're grateful for a kind word from a stranger, the perfect parking spot, or just the fact that you made it through the day, take a moment to acknowledge it. Your gratitude journal doesn't have to be perfect—it just must be a place where you celebrate the good, however small or ordinary it may seem.

4. Shift Your Perspective on Abundance

Abundance isn't just about financial wealth; it's about recognizing that life is filled with more than enough of what truly matters. Abundance is a mindset, a way of seeing the world that focuses on the richness of experiences, relationships, and opportunities rather than just the numbers in your bank account.

Try shifting your focus from scarcity, those nagging thoughts that there's never enough time, money, or love, to a mindset of abundance. Remind yourself that you have exactly what you need at this moment, and trust that more will come when the time is right. This isn't just wishful thinking; it's about aligning your mindset with the belief that the universe is inherently generous, that there's enough goodness out there for everyone, including you.

When you embrace an abundance mindset, you start to notice the countless ways in which life supports you. It could be in the form of a kind word from a friend, an unexpected opportunity, or even just the simple pleasures that bring you joy each day. Abundance is about appreciating the fullness of life in all its forms—recognizing that even when things don't go exactly as planned, there's still a wealth of experiences and possibilities available to you.

So, the next time you catch yourself thinking there's not enough, whether it's time, money, or anything else, pause and remind yourself that abundance is all around you. It's in the connections you've built, the experiences you've had, and the opportunities that continue to come your way. By shifting your focus from what's lacking to what's abundant, you open yourself up to even more of life's blessings, and you begin to see that the universe really does have your back.

5. Surround Yourself with Positivity

They say you become like the five people you spend the most time with, so choose your circle wisely. The company you keep has a profound impact on your mindset, your outlook, and even your sense of gratitude. Surround yourself with people who uplift you, who see the world through a lens of gratitude and abundance. Their positive energy will naturally rub off on you, making it easier to maintain your own sense of gratitude and appreciation for the good things in life.

Being around people who constantly focus on what's wrong, what's missing, or what could go wrong can drain your energy and dampen your spirits. But when you're in the presence of those who focus on what's right, who celebrate the small victories, and who practice gratitude regularly, it's like being in a warm, positive bubble. Their attitudes and perspectives will encourage you to see the bright side, even when things get tough.

And if you find yourself stuck with a few negative Nellies, whether they're coworkers, family members, or old friends, consider that your cue to lead by example. Your own practice of gratitude might just be contagious. By consistently expressing appreciation and focusing on the good, you might inspire them to shift their perspective as well. After all, positivity and gratitude have a way of spreading, and you never know who might catch on.

So, take a look at your inner circle and think about how they influence your mindset. Are they lifting you up, or are they pulling you down? If it's the latter, it might be time to seek out more positive influences—or better yet, become the positive influence that others need. Because at the end of the day, the energy you surround yourself with plays a huge role in shaping your outlook on life. Choose wisely and watch how your sense of gratitude and abundance flourishes.

6. Give Back

One of the most powerful ways to experience abundance is by giving to others. There's something truly magical about the act of giving, whether it's your time, your talents, or your resources. When you give, you're not just helping someone else; you're also reinforcing the idea that you have more than enough to share. It's a reminder that abundance isn't just about what you receive, but also about what you're able to give.

And the beauty of it is, giving doesn't have to be grand or extravagant to be meaningful. Small acts of kindness can have a profound impact, both on the recipient and on your own sense of abundance. Maybe it's buying a coffee for the person in line behind you or taking a few minutes out of your day to listen to a friend who needs support. It could be volunteering a few hours at a local charity or sharing your skills with someone who could benefit from them.

These small gestures not only brighten someone else's day, but they also serve as powerful reminders that you have something valuable to offer. They shift your focus away from what you might be lacking and highlight the ways in which you're already rich, rich in time, in talent, in compassion. The act of giving creates a ripple effect, spreading positivity and reinforcing the belief that abundance is all around you.

So, the next time you're feeling a bit low on abundance, try giving something away. It might be something tangible, like money or goods, or it might be something less visible but equally valuable, like your time or your attention. Whatever it is, give it freely and with an open heart, and notice how it shifts your perspective. You might just find that the more you give, the more abundant your life feels.

7. Celebrate Small Wins

Life is made up of a series of small victories, but in our hustle to reach the next big goal, we often overlook them. We tend to focus on the major milestones, thinking they're the only achievements worth celebrating. But here's the thing, those small wins? They're just as important, if not more so, because they make up the fabric of our everyday lives.

Take time to celebrate those little victories, whether it's finishing a workout, completing a project at work, or resisting the urge to eat the entire pint of ice cream (we've all been there). These moments might seem minor in the grand scheme of things, but they're proof that you're making progress, that you're moving forward. By acknowledging and celebrating these moments, you reinforce the abundance already present in your life and create a habit of seeing the good in every day.

Celebrating small victories also shifts your focus from what's still left to accomplish to what you've already achieved. It's a way of saying, "Hey, I'm doing something right here," and giving yourself a little pat on the back. And who doesn't need that from time to time?

So, the next time you complete a task, overcome a challenge, or simply make it through a tough day, take a moment to recognize it. Treat yourself to something special, share your success with a friend, or just take a deep breath and let yourself feel good about what you've done. These small celebrations create a positive feedback loop, encouraging you to keep moving forward and to appreciate the journey, not just the destination.

Because at the end of the day, life isn't just about the big wins, it's about all the small ones that add up to something truly wonderful.

8. Mindful Consumption

Be Mindful of What You Consume, and I'm Not Just Talking About Food

It's time to get real about what you're consuming and no, I don't just mean that extra-large iced coffee or the occasional late-night snack. I'm talking about everything you take in—your food, your media, your social circle, your daily conversations. Every single thing you expose yourself to has an impact on your energy, your mindset, and your well-being. So, if you're wondering why you feel drained, anxious, or stuck in a loop of negativity, it might be time to take a hard look at what you're feeding your mind, body, and soul.

Let's start with the obvious. What you eat. I'm not here to tell you to go full kale and quinoa overnight but pay attention to how certain foods make you feel. Do you feel energized, vibrant, and strong? Or are you constantly sluggish, bloated, and in a food coma by noon? Your body is your powerhouse, and if you're stuffing it full of junk, it's going to run like junk. Simple as that. Choose foods that fuel you, that make you feel alive, that support your body rather than deplete it. And no, I'm not saying you can't have your favorite treats. I'm saying find a balance that actually serves you instead of slowing you down.

Now let's talk about what you're feeding your mind. Are you constantly doom scrolling through news that makes you feel like the world is on fire? Are you following people on social media who make you feel like you're failing at life? Are you filling your head with fear, doubt, and drama instead of inspiration, learning, and growth? Your mind is a sponge. It absorbs whatever you pour into it. So be intentional about what you consume. Engage with content that lifts you up, teaches you something new, and makes you feel good.

And then there's the big one. The people you surround yourself with. Who's in your inner circle? Are they lifting you up or dragging you down? Do they celebrate your wins or secretly resent them? Do they encourage you to be the best version of yourself or do they keep you stuck in the same old patterns? The company you keep is just as important as the food you eat and the information you consume. If you're constantly surrounded by negativity, gossip, or people who drain your energy, it's going to be damn hard to feel abundant and at peace. Find your people. The ones who make you feel seen, heard, and supported. The ones who push you to grow, who call you out on your bullshit when necessary, and who remind you just how powerful you really are.

At the end of the day, what you consume physically, mentally, and emotionally shapes your entire reality. If you want to live a life that feels full, abundant, and freaking amazing, you have to start being intentional about what you allow into your space. Protect your energy. Choose your influences wisely. And remember, you are not obligated to consume anything that doesn't serve your highest good.

9. Visualize Your Abundant Life

Harnessing the Power of Visualization

Visualization is one of the most badass tools you have for manifesting abundance. And no, it's not just daydreaming about winning the lottery or picturing yourself lounging on a beach while money magically appears in your bank account (although, hey, dream big). This is about creating a mental image so vivid and so emotionally charged that your brain starts believing it's already happening.

Every day, take a few minutes to picture your life exactly as you want it. Not just the material things, but the feeling of true fulfillment, deep peace, and unshakable joy. Close your eyes and see yourself thriving. Imagine waking up in a space that feels safe and aligned with who you are. Feel the warmth of love surrounding you, the excitement of work that fuels your passion, and the sense of purpose that drives you. Picture yourself walking through life with confidence, knowing that everything you need is already on its way to you.

The secret sauce to making visualization work? Engage every damn sense. Don't just "see" it—feel it. What does it feel like to be financially secure? To be in love with someone who respects and adores you? To wake up every morning with a sense of excitement instead of dread? How does it sound when laughter fills your home? What scents are in the air when you're living your best life? The more detailed and emotionally charged your visualization is, the more your mind starts recognizing opportunities to turn it into reality.

This isn't some woo-woo, pie-in-the-sky nonsense. When you consistently practice visualization, you're literally training your brain to focus on possibilities instead of limitations. You start noticing the doors that are already open instead of the ones that are closed. You align your energy with the life you want, and in doing so, you naturally begin to make choices that move you closer to it.

So, go ahead, take a few moments every day to visualize your most abundant, joy-filled life. Let your imagination run wild. See it, feel it, and trust that the universe is already piecing together the puzzle to bring it to you. Your only job? Keep showing up for it.

Turning Challenges into Opportunities

Let's get one thing straight—life is going to throw some shit your way. There's no avoiding it. But the difference between people who stay stuck and those who thrive? It's all in how they view the challenges. Every single obstacle, setback, and "why the hell is this happening to me" moment is actually a disguised opportunity. It's a chance to grow, to evolve, to level the hell up.

Think of challenges like seeds. They might look small and insignificant at first, maybe even annoying as hell, but if you nurture them with the right mindset, they can grow into something beautiful. Every failure, every heartbreak, every misstep carries a lesson that, if learned, will set you up for something bigger and better.

So, when life kicks you in the teeth, instead of spiraling into frustration or self-pity, ask yourself: *What is this teaching me? How is this making me stronger? How can I use this experience to move forward?* Challenges aren't meant to break you; they're meant to shape you into the person you need to be to handle the abundance that's coming.

Shifting your perspective in this way does more than just make hardships bearable. It hands you back your power. Suddenly, you're not a victim of circumstance, you're the creator of your own destiny. You stop waiting for things to get better and start making them better. You take control, and that, my friend, is where real abundance begins.

Living with a Gratitude and Abundance Mindset

When you start integrating gratitude and abundance into your daily life, the world around you changes. And no, that's not just some cute, inspirational quote, it's science. Your brain starts rewiring itself to focus on what's working instead of what's lacking. You begin to see opportunities where you once saw roadblocks. You attract more of what you're putting out into the universe.

Imagine waking up each day not dreading what's ahead but actually feeling excited. Imagine feeling grateful not just for the big, flashy moments but for the little things, the way your morning coffee warms your hands, the way the sun hits your face, the way a friend makes you laugh so hard you snort. This mindset shift doesn't just change how you experience life; it changes what life brings you in return.

Because here's the truth, what you focus on expands. If you're always focused on what's missing, what's wrong, what's not enough, guess what? That's what you'll keep getting more of. But if you focus on what's good, what's growing, what's already abundant in your life, that energy multiplies.

So, take a deep breath, look around, and recognize the blessings already in front of you. Trust that more is coming. Know that you don't have to chase abundance, it's already within you, just waiting for you to claim it. Keep your heart open, your mindset strong, and watch how the universe rises to meet you.

Gratitude as a Spiritual Practice

Gratitude as a spiritual practice isn't just about tossing out a quick "thank you" when someone holds the door open for you, though basic manners are always a plus. It's about making gratitude a way of life, an intentional act of appreciation that weaves itself into everything you do. Think of it as the golden thread that connects you to something greater, whether you call it the universe, divine energy, or just the rhythm of life itself.

When you make gratitude a spiritual practice, you're not just checking off a mental list of things you're thankful for. You're actively shifting your focus from what's missing to what's already abundant in your life. It's about seeing the sacred in the mundane—a deep breath of fresh air, the warmth of a morning sunbeam, the sound of laughter with a friend. These little moments, when fully acknowledged, become powerful reminders of how much beauty already surrounds you.

The Transformative Power of Gratitude

Gratitude isn't just a fluffy, feel-good emotion; it's a powerful tool for transformation. When you commit to a gratitude practice, you're training your mind to look for the good, even when life is throwing curveballs. This shift in perspective is what separates those who thrive from those who stay stuck in negativity. Life will always have challenges, but when you can still find gratitude in the storm, you build resilience, peace, and a deep trust that things are unfolding as they should.

This isn't about ignoring pain or hardship. It's about realizing that even in difficult times, there's something to hold onto. Maybe it's the strength you're developing, the lesson you're learning, or the person standing beside you when you need them most. Gratitude allows you to acknowledge struggle without letting it define you. It's like having an emotional anchor that keeps you steady, even when the waters get rough.

Gratitude and Presence

One of the sneakiest ways we sabotage our happiness is by constantly chasing the next big thing. The next goal, the next milestone, the next upgrade. Society thrives on keeping us in a state of "never enough," convincing us that fulfillment is just one achievement away. Gratitude, on the other hand, invites you to pause, breathe, and recognize that you already have so much to be grateful for right here, right now.

By practicing gratitude, you step into the present moment with more awareness. You stop waiting for happiness to come *after* something happens and start experiencing it in real time. This doesn't mean you stop striving for more, but it does mean you stop postponing your joy until you reach some arbitrary finish line. The truth is, if you can't appreciate what you have now, you won't magically become grateful once you get more. Gratitude is a muscle—you have to work it daily.

Gratitude Deepens Connection

If you want to strengthen your relationships, start practicing gratitude. Nothing makes people feel more valued and appreciated than knowing they matter. When you acknowledge the impact, someone has on your life—whether it's a friend who always shows up, a partner who supports your dreams, or even a stranger who gave you a kind smile on a rough day—you create deeper bonds. Gratitude shifts your focus from what people *aren't* doing to everything they *are* doing, which fosters a sense of love, community, and belonging.

It also works both ways. When you make a habit of expressing gratitude, people naturally feel drawn to you. Nobody likes to be around someone who constantly complains or takes everything for granted. But someone who genuinely appreciates the little things? That energy is magnetic. Gratitude is the kind of thing that spreads. The more you practice it; the more others are inspired to do the same.

How to Make Gratitude a Daily Practice

Incorporating gratitude into your daily life doesn't have to be complicated. You don't need to carve out hours of meditation time or write pages of gratitude lists (unless you want to). It can be as simple as:

- Taking 30 seconds every morning to acknowledge one thing you're grateful for.
- Sending a quick message to someone to let them know you appreciate them.
- Reflecting on three things that made you smile before you go to bed.
- Saying "thank you" with genuine presence, not just as a reflex.
- Keeping a gratitude jar and adding notes about moments that make your heart full.

The goal is to make gratitude a natural part of your mindset, not just an occasional practice. The more you train yourself to see the good, the easier it becomes to live in a state of appreciation.

Living with a Grateful Heart

At the end of the day, gratitude is a choice. You can choose to see what's missing, or you can choose to see what's already here. You can focus on what went wrong, or you can focus on the lesson it taught you. You can dwell on the struggles, or you can recognize the strength you gained from them.

When you embrace gratitude as a spiritual practice, you shift from surviving to truly *living*. You stop waiting for the perfect conditions and start seeing the magic in the mess. You open yourself up to more joy, more peace, and more abundance—not because your circumstances change, but because *you* do.

So, take a deep breath, look around, and find something—anything—to be grateful for. Let that gratitude fill your heart and watch how it transforms the way you experience life.

The Transformative Power of Gratitude in Daily Life

Gratitude has the power to flip your life on its head in the best way possible. It's like that one friend who always knows how to turn a shitty situation into a lesson or a laugh. When you start shifting your focus from what's missing to what's already present, life doesn't feel so damn heavy. Suddenly, instead of obsessing over what you don't have, you start realizing just how much you do—and that shift alone is enough to change everything.

Gratitude isn't just about tossing out a polite "thanks" when someone holds the door or nails your coffee order. It's about rewiring your perspective to notice the gold nuggets in life—even when it feels like the universe just dumped a cosmic junk drawer in your lap. It shifts your mindset, making it easier to find joy in the everyday—a peaceful morning, a soul-filling conversation, or just surviving the chaos without completely unraveling. When you start soaking in the beauty of the now, life gets deeper, more colorful, and way more satisfying.

One of the biggest ways gratitude flips the script is in your relationships. When you intentionally recognize the people who show up for you, root for you, or simply brighten your day, those connections grow stronger. Appreciation is emotional glue. Whether it's your partner, a ride-or-die friend, or the coworker who remembers you hate meetings before 10 a.m., people want to feel valued. And let's face it, few things diffuse drama faster than a sincere "I'm thankful for you" when things get tense.

Now, if you're sitting here thinking, "Yeah, yeah, I get it, gratitude is good, but life is still a mess," I hear you. Practicing gratitude doesn't mean pretending everything is sunshine and rainbows when it's clearly a dumpster fire. It means acknowledging the good *even when* the fire is burning. It's about recognizing that there's always something to hold onto, even if it's just the fact that you made it through another day. That alone is worth some gratitude.

Gratitude in Action

So, how do you make gratitude a daily habit without feeling like you're forcing it? Easy. You sneak it into your life like a little ritual—something that becomes second nature. Try these simple ways to cultivate more gratitude without making it a chore:

- **Morning Gratitude Check:** Before your feet hit the floor, name three things you're grateful for. Even if it's just "I woke up," "I have coffee," and "I don't have to deal with Karen from accounting today," it counts.
- **Gratitude Jar:** Keep a jar where you jot down little wins or happy moments throughout the week. Then, on days when life feels like a mess, pull one out and remind yourself that good things *do* happen.
- **Verbal Appreciation:** Actually, *tell* people when you appreciate them. A quick "Hey, I love how you always check in on me" or "I really appreciate you" goes a long way.
- **Gratitude Walks:** Take a few minutes each day to step outside and just *notice* what's around you. The sun, the breeze, the way the trees move—gratitude isn't just about the big stuff.

By making gratitude a habit, you're not just changing your mindset; you're changing the energy you put out into the world. And trust me, the universe notices when you start paying attention to the good.

Affirmations for Cultivating Gratitude

If you want to supercharge your gratitude practice, affirmations can help keep you on track. Try these whenever you need a reset:

- "I am grateful for the abundance in my life, seen and unseen."
- "With each breath, I welcome gratitude and let go of what no longer serves me."
- "I cherish the beauty in the simple moments and find joy in the everyday."
- "Gratitude flows through me, guiding me toward more joy and fulfillment."
- "I acknowledge the lessons in every challenge and am thankful for the growth they bring."
- "I am surrounded by love, support, and opportunities for happiness."

Now, let's dive into abundance because gratitude and abundance are like besties—they go hand in hand.

Abundance Mindset: Stop Hoarding Your Cake

An abundance mindset is like switching from a black-and-white TV to full-blown 4K HDR. It changes *everything*. Instead of waking up thinking, *there's never enough—money, time, opportunities, patience* (especially patience), you start seeing life as a giant buffet where there's plenty to go around.

But let's be real, shifting to an abundance mindset doesn't mean you suddenly have stacks of cash falling from the sky or that everything magically works out in your favor overnight. It's about retraining your brain to believe that good things are available to *you*—not just the lucky few. It's about realizing that someone else's success doesn't take away from yours and that opportunities aren't scarce, they're just waiting for you to claim them.

Think back to being a kid with birthday cake. You'd get that one slice and guard it like a dragon hoarding gold, terrified it was the last piece of cake you'd ever see. But imagine if someone came along and said, "Relax, there's an entire bakery out back." That's what an abundance mindset does. It stops you from living in fear of lack and instead lets you enjoy what you have, knowing more is always on the way.

Flipping the Scarcity Script

We've been conditioned to believe there's never enough—whether it's time, money, success, or even love. That's some deep programming to undo, but it's possible. The next time you catch yourself thinking, *there's not enough* (money, love, luck, whatever), pause and reframe. Try:

- Instead of "I'll never have enough money," say, "Money flows to me in expected and unexpected ways."
- Instead of "I don't have enough time," say, "I have enough time for what truly matters."
- Instead of "I'll never be as successful as them," say, "Their success shows me what's possible for me too."

And yes, this takes practice. You might not believe these statements at first, but the more you say them, the more your brain starts accepting them as truth.

Attracting More Abundance

The wild thing about abundance? The more you give, the more you get. The universe has this funny way of matching your energy, so when you start acting like there's plenty to go around—whether it's love, opportunities, kindness—you start seeing more of it.

Here's how to invite more abundance into your life:

- **Stop keeping score.** Give without expecting immediate returns. Whether it's time, support, or even a compliment, when you give freely, the universe takes note.

- **Surround yourself with an abundant mindset.** Hang out with people who lift you up, who see possibilities instead of limits. Energy is contagious—make sure you're catching the right kind.
- **Say yes to opportunities.** Stop waiting for the "perfect" moment. Sometimes, abundance shows up disguised as a risk.
- **Celebrate others.** Their success doesn't take away from yours. In fact, it's proof that abundance is real and accessible.

At the end of the day, an abundance mindset isn't about having everything—it's about *believing* you have access to everything you need. So, stop hoarding your slice of cake, my friend. There's an entire damn bakery out there, and it's got your name written all over it.

Shifting from Scarcity to Abundance

Shifting from a scarcity mindset to one of abundance is like upgrading from an old, glitchy flip phone to the latest iPhone—you didn't even realize how much you were missing until you made the switch. It changes everything. Your relationships, your career, your finances, your entire outlook on life. But let's be real, this isn't some "wake up and suddenly feel rich" kind of transformation. It takes effort. It takes intention. And most of all, it takes being willing to see the world differently.

When you're stuck in scarcity mode, life feels like an endless competition. There's never enough—never enough time, money, success, love, or luck. It's like you're always waiting for the other shoe to drop, convinced that if someone else is winning, it must mean you're losing. And that kind of thinking? It's exhausting. It keeps you in survival mode, hoarding your energy, your resources, and sometimes even your love, because deep down, you're terrified there won't be more.

But here's the truth: Abundance isn't about what's in your bank account or how much stuff you have. It's a mindset. It's the belief that the universe isn't stingy, that there is more than enough success, love, and happiness to go around—and that you're fully deserving of your share. When you shift to an abundance mindset, everything starts to look different. Instead of seeing dead ends, you see opportunities. Instead of holding on for dear life, you trust that what's meant for you will find its way.

So how do you start making this shift? You start questioning every lie that scarcity has told you.

When you hear yourself thinking, *I'll never have enough money,* stop and reframe it. Ask yourself, *Is that actually true? Or is it just a belief I've been carrying?* Money, like energy, flows where attention goes. If you believe you'll never have enough, you'll act in ways that reinforce that belief. If you start believing there's always a way, suddenly, you begin to see options where you once saw roadblocks.

This shift isn't just about money—it's about everything. In relationships, it means giving love freely instead of withholding it out of fear. It means supporting others without feeling like their success takes away from yours. In your career, it might mean stepping out of your comfort zone, trusting that the right opportunities will find you when you take action. It's about loosening the death grip of control and learning to trust in life's flow.

And let's be honest, shifting from scarcity to abundance isn't something that happens overnight. It's a practice. A conscious decision every single day to believe that the universe is more generous than we give it credit for. Once you start seeing the world this way, you'll wonder how you ever lived any other way.

Exercises to Shift into Abundance Mode

Alright, now that we've called out scarcity for the lying little gremlin that it is, let's dive into some real, practical ways to shift your mindset. Think of these exercises as your toolkit for rewiring your brain for gratitude, joy, and, most importantly, *abundance.*

1. Daily Gratitude Journal

What to do: Every morning or night, write down at least three things you're grateful for. Could be something small, like your first sip of coffee, or something big, like a major win at work.

Why it works: When you train your brain to look for what's *already* good, you start naturally attracting more good. Simple as that.

2. Write a Gratitude Letter

What to do: Once a week, write a letter to someone who has impacted your life—friend, mentor, coworker, hell, even your mail carrier. Then send it.

Why it works: Expressing gratitude not only strengthens your relationships but also reminds you just how much love and support you *already* have.

3. Abundance Affirmations

What to do: Create a list of affirmations that reinforce abundance. Say them out loud every morning, even if you feel ridiculous at first. Some examples:

- *I am open to receiving the endless opportunities life offers me.*
- *There is more than enough success, money, and happiness to go around.*
- *I attract abundance effortlessly.*

Why it works: Your subconscious listens to what you tell it. Keep feeding it thoughts of abundance, and eventually, it'll start acting accordingly.

4. The Abundance Jar

What to do: Find a jar and every time something good happens—big or small—write it down and throw it in. On tough days, pull a note out and remind yourself of how much abundance already exists in your life.

Why it works: This is a physical, visual reminder that good things are always happening, even when life tries to convince you otherwise.

5. Scarcity to Abundance Reframe

What to do: Every time you catch yourself thinking a scarcity-based thought, pause and flip the script.

- Instead of *I never have enough time,* say *I always have enough time for what truly matters.*
- Instead of *I'll never be able to afford that,* say *Money is always flowing to me in new and unexpected ways.*

Why it works: It forces you to break the scarcity cycle and start focusing on possibility instead of limitation.

6. Visualization Practice

What to do: Spend five minutes a day visualizing your most abundant life. Picture yourself living in total financial freedom, feeling deeply loved, waking up excited for your day. Imagine it in full detail—what does it smell like, sound like, feel like?

Why it works: Your brain doesn't know the difference between real and imagined experiences. The more you "experience" abundance in your mind, the more your actions start aligning to make it your reality.

7. Generosity as a Path to Abundance

What to do: Give something every day—whether it's your time, energy, knowledge, or even just a compliment.

Why it works: Scarcity tells you to hoard. Abundance knows there's always more. The more you give, the more you reinforce that belief in yourself.

Wrapping It Up: Living in Abundance

Shifting into an abundance mindset isn't just about *getting more*—it's about realizing you *already have more than enough* to start living a fulfilled, joyful life. It's about rewiring yourself to focus on opportunities instead of limitations, on gratitude instead of what's missing.

That doesn't mean life suddenly becomes perfect. Challenges will still show up, people will still be frustrating, and sometimes, you'll still wish you had more money in your bank account. But when you're living in an abundance mindset, none of that holds the same power over you. Because you know deep down that no matter what happens, there's always more love, more success, more joy, and more opportunity waiting for you.

So, start today. Start now. Train your brain to look for the abundance around you, and I promise, the more you seek it, the more you'll find. And above all, don't forget to enjoy the ride—after all, what's the point of abundance if you're not having a damn good time along the way?

Chapter 8

Embracing Change and Transformation

*"Embracing change is the gateway to transformation;
it's in the surrender to the unknown that we uncover
our greatest growth and discover the beauty of who
we're becoming."* —Jamie

The Unpredictable, Chaotic, Beautiful Mess of Change

Let's be real. Change is about as welcome as stepping barefoot onto a rogue LEGO. It is inconvenient. It is uncomfortable. It messes with your plans and forces you out of your cozy little comfort zone where things are predictable and safe. But here is the thing. Just like that unexpected rainstorm that soaks you to the bone but leads you to the best coffee shop you never knew existed, change has a sneaky way of shaking things up in the best possible way—*if* you are willing to stop fighting it and start *flowing* with it.

In this chapter, we are diving headfirst into the swirling, unpredictable waters of transformation. We are talking about those moments that knock the wind out of you, the ones that force you to take a hard look at your life and ask, *What the hell am I doing?* Because let's be honest. Most of us do not wake up one day and say, *You know what sounds fun? Completely uprooting my life and becoming a new version of myself!* No. Change usually sneaks up on you when you least expect it, flipping everything upside down until you have no choice but to adapt.

Transformation is not just about changing your circumstances. It is about shifting your mindset, your perspective, and ultimately, the way you show up for yourself. It is about recognizing when the life you have built no longer fits and having the courage to let go of what is no longer serving you. And yes, it is terrifying. Yes, it is messy. And yes, it will probably make you question everything at least once. But the truth is, every time we are faced with change, we have two choices: to cling desperately to the past out of fear, or to step forward into the unknown with curiosity, trust, and maybe even a little excitement.

Throughout this chapter, we are going to explore how to navigate change with grace and resilience. We are going to talk about how to let go of the things that keep you stuck, how to embrace uncertainty without spiraling into full-blown panic, and how to cultivate the courage to reinvent yourself when life demands it. And of course, we are going to do it all with a solid dose of humor, because if there is one thing that makes change a little less terrifying, it is the ability to laugh at life's complete disregard for your carefully laid plans.

So grab your metaphorical rain boots, because we are about to wade into the messy, beautiful, transformative process of change. You might just find that instead of drowning, you are learning to *dance* through it. Because transformation is not just about what you lose—it is about what you *gain* in the process. Strength. Wisdom. Self-awareness. And the undeniable proof that you are capable of handling *whatever* life throws your way.

When Life Smacks You With a Wake-Up Call

The thing about change is that it does not give a damn about your schedule. It does not wait for you to be ready before it turns your world inside out. But here is the secret most people do not talk about. That chaos? That complete unraveling of everything you thought was solid? That is where the magic happens.

Because transformation, when embraced, is not just about survival. It is about stepping into a version of yourself that is stronger, wiser, and more in tune with your soul's purpose. It is in those moments of upheaval that we learn what we are really made of. We realize how much we can handle. We grow in ways we never thought possible.

So let me ask you. Where in your life are you feeling the pull for change? What areas are whispering—or let's be real, *screaming*—for you to evolve? And the most important question of all, are you willing to trust that whatever is falling apart is doing so to make room for something *better*?

Because here is the truth. Embracing change is not just about getting through it. It is about allowing it to shape you into the person you were always meant to become. And while the road might be winding, unpredictable, and full of moments that make you want to scream into the void, it is also leading you exactly where you are meant to be.

My Own Transformation: From Self-Destruction to Self-Discovery

I remember the moment I realized my life *had* to change. It was not some grand Hollywood-style revelation with dramatic music playing in the background. No lightning bolts of inspiration. Just a slow, nagging whisper that grew louder and louder until I could not ignore it anymore.

I had spent years stuck in cycles of pain and self-destruction, buried under the weight of my past, my addictions, and the stories I kept telling myself about who I was. But there came a point where I had to face the truth. If I did not change, I was going to lose myself completely.

So I did the hardest thing I have ever done. I *chose* change.

Through trauma therapy, I dug deep into the wounds I had carried for so long. I turned inward. I explored my spirituality. I reconnected with a version of myself that had been buried for years under all the pain, all the self-doubt, all the survival mode bullshit. Slowly but surely, I started to see my worth. I started to let go of my addictions. I started to believe that maybe, just maybe, I was meant for *more* than just surviving.

And as I healed, something unexpected happened. A new energy bubbled up inside of me—one I had not felt in years. It was the drive to *create*. To turn my pain into something meaningful. To build something positive out of the ashes of my old life. The more I worked on myself, the more I felt called to help others on their journeys.

That is when I realized my purpose.

I was meant to guide others through their own transformations. To use my experiences, my lessons, and my scars to help people navigate their own healing. So I stepped fully into my role as a spiritual life coach. I started helping others connect with their inner selves, heal their pasts, and step into their own power.

Rewriting My Story—And Helping Others Do the Same

Looking back, it is surreal to see how far I have come. I went from being trapped in a cycle of addiction and self-doubt to building a life I am *damn* proud of. A life where I get to help others find their own paths to healing and empowerment. My past no longer defines me. It has shaped me, but it does not *own* me.

I have stepped into a new way of living. One filled with purpose, passion, and the undeniable knowing that transformation is *always* possible. No matter how lost you feel. No matter how many times you have fallen. No matter how much your past tries to convince you that you are stuck.

You are not.

You are evolving. You are healing. And you are stepping into the version of yourself that you were always meant to be.

And trust me, you are just getting started.

The Nature of Change

Now it is time to talk about the nature of change. Change is the only constant in life, a phrase you have probably heard a thousand times, and each time it might have made you want to roll your eyes just a little bit more. But like it or not, it is the truth. Change is inevitable, unpredictable, and often comes without warning, like an uninvited guest barging in to rearrange your furniture and throw your plans out the window. We do not always welcome it, but the reality is, change is not just necessary. It is the very thing that keeps us growing.

Change has a mind of its own. Sometimes it is a gentle breeze, shifting things in a way that feels natural and easy. Other times, it is a full-blown hurricane that knocks the breath out of you and leaves you scrambling to figure out what just happened. But just like storms eventually clear and give way to blue skies, the changes we face, whether small adjustments or life-altering transformations, always have the potential to lead us somewhere better. That is, if we stop fighting them and start flowing with them.

Understanding that change is unavoidable is one of the most freeing realizations you can have on this wild soul's journey. Imagine life as a river, constantly moving and never stagnant. You cannot step into the same river twice because the water is always shifting, just like we are. The secret to making peace with change is not to build a dam and resist the current. It is to learn how to move with it, even when it twists and turns in ways you never expected.

Change, though often uncomfortable, is how we grow. It is the universe's way of nudging us, or, let's be honest, sometimes shoving us, toward our next level of evolution. Think about the caterpillar transforming into a butterfly. It does not sit there complaining about how hard metamorphosis is. It surrenders to the process, knowing that something greater is on the other side. In the same way, our lives are a series of transformations, each one bringing us closer to who we are meant to be.

Let's be honest. Embracing change is rarely a smooth and effortless process. It can be terrifying, messy, and at times, it hurts like hell. But when we stop seeing change as something to be feared and start seeing it as an opportunity, everything shifts. Instead of asking why this is happening, we start asking what this is trying to teach us and how we can grow from the experience.

When we begin to approach change with curiosity instead of resistance, it stops feeling like the enemy. Instead, it becomes an ally, one that pushes us toward greater understanding. compassion, and wisdom.

The soul's journey is not about staying the same. It is about evolving. It is about learning. It is about stepping into deeper alignment with who you truly are. Every shift, no matter how small or disruptive, is a step forward. And when we stop fighting change and start trusting it, life has a way of leading us exactly where we are meant to be.

Personal Transformation: The Soul's Version of a Major Glow-Up

Personal transformation is not just about switching up your hairstyle or upgrading your wardrobe. This is not some surface-level makeover. This is a full-blown, soul-deep renovation. It is peeling back layers, tearing down outdated structures, and rebuilding from the inside out. It is knocking down the walls of old beliefs, clearing out the emotional junk drawer, and finally realizing that you were never meant to stay stuck in a version of yourself that no longer fits.

But let's be honest. Transformation is not some graceful, cinematic moment where the music swells, and everything suddenly falls into place. It is messy. It is uncomfortable. It is the emotional equivalent of deciding to deep-clean your entire house, only to find yourself three hours in, surrounded by chaos, wondering why you started in the first place. But here is where the magic happens. That discomfort? That chaos? That is proof that something is shifting.

Transformation is not about becoming someone new. It is about uncovering the person you have always been but somehow lost sight of along the way. It is about peeling off the layers that society, past trauma, and your own self-doubt have piled on top of you. And while it might not always be pretty, it is *necessary*. Because you cannot step into your fullest, most authentic self if you are still dragging around the weight of who you *used* to be.

So, consider this process your personal, soul-level spring cleaning. You are clearing out the clutter, letting go of what no longer serves you, and making space for something better. Yes, it is going to push you out of your comfort zone. Yes, it might feel like you are navigating a maze blindfolded while wearing heels two sizes too small. But that is where the real growth happens. When you are stretched, challenged, and forced to confront the parts of yourself you would rather avoid, that is when you discover just how strong, resilient, and capable you truly are.

Now, if you are staring at your life thinking, *Okay, but where the hell do I even start?*, do not worry. I have got you. The steps I am about to share

are not some magical formula that will make transformation easy, but they will help you move through it with clarity, confidence, and maybe even a little excitement. So, take a deep breath, shake off the self-doubt, and let's break this down.

The Roadmap to Your Personal Transformation

1. Admit That Something Needs to Change

The first step to any transformation is getting brutally honest with yourself. If you are feeling stuck, unfulfilled, or just know in your gut that something is *off*, do not ignore it. That feeling is not there to torture you; it is trying to wake you up. Acknowledge it without judgment. It is not about blaming yourself for where you are—it is about recognizing that you are ready for something *more*.

2. Set Intentions, Not Unrealistic Goals

People love setting massive, rigid goals and then wonder why they feel like failures when life does not go according to plan. Instead of saying, "I am going to completely change my life in six months," try setting an intention: "I am committed to making choices that align with my happiness and well-being." Intentions keep you open to different paths while still guiding you in the right direction.

3. Give Yourself Some Damn Grace

Transformation is not a straight line. There will be detours. There will be setbacks. There will be days when you feel like you are back at square one, wondering why you even bothered. That is normal. Growth is not about perfection—it is about persistence. Be kind to yourself in the messy middle. Celebrate progress, even if it is tiny.

4. Stay Present Instead of Obsessing Over the Finish Line

If you are constantly focused on where you *should* be, you will miss the lessons that are happening *right now*. Instead of stressing about the final destination, ground yourself in the present. Meditation, journaling, or just taking five minutes to breathe can help you stay connected to the journey rather than rushing to the outcome.

5. Stop Being Afraid of the Unknown

The unknown is terrifying. It is also where the best things in life happen. If you wait until you have every detail figured out before taking action, you will stay exactly where you are. Trust that even if you cannot see the full path, each step forward is leading you somewhere you are meant to be.

6. Find Your Support System

You do not have to do this alone. Whether it is a mentor, a therapist, or that one brutally honest friend who tells you what you *need* to hear, surround yourself with people who lift you up and hold you accountable. Transformation is tough, but having the right people in your corner makes it a hell of a lot easier.

7. Let Go of the Baggage That is Holding You Back

Old habits, toxic relationships, limiting beliefs—if it is not serving your growth, it has got to go. And yes, that might mean making some hard choices. But the truth is, you cannot step into your highest self while dragging around the weight of everything that is keeping you small.

8. Celebrate Every Step Forward

Stop waiting until you have reached some imaginary finish line to be proud of yourself. Every time you choose growth over comfort, every time you face a fear, every time you take even the smallest step forward—that is worth celebrating. Give yourself credit. You are doing the work.

You Are Already in the Process of Transforming

If you have read this far, guess what? You have already started. That means you are ready to do the work, to face the uncomfortable, and to step into the version of yourself that you were always meant to be.

And here is the best part. You do not have to have it all figured out right now. Transformation is not about flipping a switch and suddenly becoming a brand-new person. It is about gradual shifts, small victories, and embracing the process as it unfolds.

So, keep going. Keep trusting. Keep showing up for yourself. Because every choice you make to grow, to heal, and to step into your power brings you closer to the life you were always meant to live.

And believe me—you are just getting started.

Exercises: Reflecting on Your Past Transformations and Envisioning Your Future Glow-Up

Think of your life as a book, except instead of a neatly plotted novel, it is more like a choose-your-own-adventure with unexpected twists, questionable decisions, and the occasional "WTF was I thinking?" moment. Some chapters you might want to re-read and cherish, while others? Straight to the *do not recommend* pile. But here is the deal—every messy, beautiful, painful, and triumphant page has shaped the person you are today.

These exercises are here to help you look back at those pivotal moments, the ones that cracked you open and forced you to grow, the ones that changed you in ways you never saw coming. But we are not just reminiscing about the past. We are looking ahead, plotting out the next epic chapter of your life. Because your story is far from over, and you, my friend, are the one holding the pen.

So, let's dive in. These exercises will help you reflect on where you have been, acknowledge how far you have come, and set a clear vision for the badass you are becoming.

1. The Transformation Timeline

Objective: See the bigger picture of your growth by mapping out the major transformations you have experienced.

Instructions: Draw out a timeline of your life. Mark the key events, challenges, or turning points where you experienced major change. For each one, ask yourself:

- What triggered this transformation?
- How did I respond to it?
- What did I learn?
- How has it shaped the person I am today?

This is your proof that you have already conquered change before. You have been through the fire and come out stronger every time. Take a moment to really acknowledge that.

2. A Love Letter to Your Past Self

Objective: Show compassion to the version of you that had to fight to get here.

Instructions: Write a letter to yourself at a time when you were struggling through a big change. Maybe it was when you were lost, scared, or doubting your strength. Offer that past version of you the wisdom, encouragement, and kindness you *wish* you had back then. Tell them how proud you are of their resilience. Thank them for pushing through. Remind them that every painful moment led to something greater.

And while you are at it, give yourself credit for making it to the other side. You earned it.

3. Future Visioning: Who Is the Next Version of You?

Objective: Get clear on what you want your next transformation to look like.

Instructions: Close your eyes and picture your future self. Not just what you look like, but how you *feel*. How do you carry yourself? What energy do you radiate? What goals have you accomplished? Who have you become?

Now, write it all down. Describe this future version of yourself in vivid detail. And then ask yourself:

- What steps do I need to take today to start becoming that person?
- What habits, mindsets, or people do I need to let go of?
- What is one thing I can do right now to move toward that vision?

This is not about waiting for the "perfect moment." It is about making intentional choices *right now* to create the future you deserve.

4. Transformation Gratitude Journal

Objective: Shift your perspective by appreciating the changes that have helped you grow.

Instructions: Dedicate a section of your journal to listing the transformations you are grateful for. Think about the changes that, even if they were painful at the time, led to something better. Write about how they shaped you, what they taught you, and why you would not be the person you are today without them.

Because sometimes, the hardest changes turn out to be the greatest gifts. And gratitude has a way of making even the messy parts feel a little more meaningful.

5. Mapping Your Next Steps: Turning Reflection into Action

Objective: Break down your next transformation into practical, doable steps.

Instructions: Based on your reflections and your future vision, create a roadmap for where you want to go next.

- List out the changes you want to make.
- Break them down into smaller, realistic steps.
- Set a timeline (but stay flexible, because life loves throwing surprises).
- Identify what resources, habits, or support systems will help you along the way.

Think of it like GPS for your transformation. You might take a few detours, but as long as you keep moving forward, you *will* get there.

Your Transformation Is Still Unfolding

As we wrap up this chapter, it is important to remember that transformation is not a one-time event. It is not something you cross off your to-do list and call it a day. It is an ongoing, ever-evolving journey.

Each shift, no matter how small, is another thread in the tapestry of your life. Some changes will feel subtle. Others will feel like a damn wrecking ball knocking down everything you thought you knew. But all of them are shaping you into the person you are meant to be.

So, keep reflecting. Keep growing. Keep stepping boldly into your next evolution.

Because your story? It is still being written. And the next chapter? It is going to be *legendary*.

Remember, embracing change is about more than just going with the flow—it's about actively choosing to evolve, to learn from your experiences, and to continually strive to become the best version of yourself. Whether you're reflecting on past transformations or envisioning future growth, know that each step you take is a step toward greater self-awareness, fulfillment, and alignment with your soul's purpose.

So, as you move forward, keep an open heart and mind. Embrace the changes that come your way, knowing that they're guiding you toward something greater. Trust in your ability to navigate whatever life throws at you, and don't be afraid to write new chapters in your story—chapters that are filled with possibility, growth, and the realization of your deepest desires. After all, the journey of transformation is one of the most profound and rewarding paths you'll ever walk.

Chapter 9

Embracing Joy and Playfulness in Life

"Joy and playfulness are the sparkles of life. When we embrace them, we invite the magic of everyday moments to dance and light up our world." —Jamie

The Power of Play: Why Joy is Non-Negotiable

Life can feel like one never-ending to-do list. Bills, deadlines, responsibilities, and the never-ending pressure to have it all figured out. Somewhere between childhood and adulthood, most of us swapped playdates for productivity and belly laughs for burnout. But who said growing up meant growing out of joy?

This chapter is your permission slip to stop taking life so damn seriously and start having *fun* again. Not just the occasional night out or the rare vacation, but the kind of everyday joy that makes life worth living. Because here is the truth—play is not just for kids. It is a survival skill. It is the reset button for your soul. It is the thing that keeps you from turning into a stress ball of anxiety and resentment.

Why Play is Not Just Fun, But Essential

Remember when your biggest worry was what game to play next? When you could lose yourself in make-believe worlds, laugh until your stomach hurt, and see adventure in the simplest of things? Somewhere along the way, adulthood happened, and most of us traded in that magic for a never-ending cycle of work, stress, and obligations. But here is the secret—*you never actually lost that part of you.* You just buried it under layers of "shoulds" and "musts."

Joy and play are not frivolous. They are not luxuries for people who have extra time on their hands. They are essential to a fulfilling, balanced life. When you embrace playfulness, you:

Reduce stress – Laughter literally lowers cortisol levels and reminds you that not everything is an emergency.

Boost creativity – Some of the best ideas come when you are relaxed and having fun. Ever noticed how kids are natural artists, inventors, and storytellers? That is because play unlocks *limitless* creativity.

Strengthen relationships – Play helps you connect, whether it is through shared laughter, inside jokes, or spontaneous adventures. People bond through fun, not just serious conversations.

Feel more alive – When you stop living in "get-through-the-day" mode and start actually *enjoying* life, everything shifts.

So, if you have been feeling uninspired, overwhelmed, or just kind of *meh* about life, play is not something you should squeeze in *if* you have time. It is something you need to prioritize *now.*

How to Reignite Your Playful Spirit

If the idea of adding more play into your life feels like just *another* thing to do, do not worry—I am not here to hand you another homework assignment. Think of this as a reminder to bring more ease, fun, and laughter into your *existing* life.

Here is how to make that happen:

1. Give Yourself Permission to Play

Seriously, let go of the guilt. Play is *not* a waste of time. It is self-care, healing, and sometimes even the thing that saves you from completely losing your mind. The more you embrace joy, the more energy you will have for the "serious" stuff.

2. Find What Lights You Up

What did you *love* to do as a kid? Did you love drawing, dancing, building things, or pretending to be a rockstar in your bedroom? Chances are, there is a version of that joy still waiting for you. Reconnect with hobbies that have nothing to do with making money or being productive. Just have fun for the sake of it.

3. Make Fun a Daily Habit

Joy should not be reserved for vacations and weekends. Find small ways to inject fun into your everyday routine. Play your favorite music while cooking, crack jokes with your coworkers, or turn your daily walk into a mini-adventure by taking a new route.

4. Stop Worrying About Looking Silly

One of the biggest blocks to playfulness? Fear of what people will think. Guess what? No one actually cares. And if they do, they probably need a little more playfulness in *their* life. Dance like a weirdo, try that hobby you have always wanted to, wear the ridiculous outfit that makes you happy. Life is too short to be serious all the time.

5. Surround Yourself with Playful People

Ever notice how some people just *radiate* joy? Those are the people you want in your life. Find friends who make you laugh, who bring out your adventurous side, and who remind you that fun is a priority, not an afterthought.

6. Laugh More, Worry Less

Laughter is literally healing. Watch that ridiculous comedy, swap memes with friends, and learn to laugh at the absurdity of life instead of letting it stress you out. If you can laugh about it, you can get through it.

It is Time to Bring the Fun Back

This chapter is your reminder that life is not meant to be one long to-do list. It is meant to be lived, enjoyed, and savored. Play is not irresponsible. It is not childish. It is one of the most powerful things you can do for your mind, body, and soul.

So, what are you waiting for? Turn up the music. Try something new. Laugh until your cheeks hurt. Because when you start prioritizing joy, everything else in life starts feeling *a whole lot lighter*.

The Transformative Power of Play: Because Life is Meant to Be Lived, Not Just Managed

Play is not just something kids do to pass the time. It is a superpower, a stress-buster, a creativity booster, and quite possibly the thing that is missing from your life right now. When was the last time you truly let loose and played? Not just a little laugh here and there, but full-on, bellyaching, carefree fun? Whether it is a ridiculous dance party in your living room, a prank war with a friend, or just being silly for no damn reason, play has the power to shake you out of your daily grind and reconnect you with a version of yourself that is actually enjoying life.

Play is not just about having fun. It is about rewiring your brain to see the world differently. It flips a switch, shifting you from stress mode to creativity mode, from overthinking to just being. Play helps you loosen your grip on life's endless pressures, and as a bonus, it can actually make you better at dealing with the hard stuff. When you play, you access a different part of your brain, the part that is curious, open, and able to see solutions that stress would have blinded you to.

Play is also a connection builder. When you share laughter and fun with someone, you form deeper bonds, strengthen relationships, and create moments that make life feel lighter. And let's be honest, we could all use a little more of that.

If you have been feeling overwhelmed, uninspired, or like you are just going through the motions, it is time to inject some play into your life. Not as an afterthought, not as a luxury, but as a non-negotiable. Because life is not meant to be all work and no fun. It is meant to be lived.

How to Bring More Playfulness into Your Life

1. Make Play a Priority, Not an Afterthought

If you do not make time for fun, life will fill your schedule with obligations, stress, and a never-ending list of things that need to get done.

- Schedule it. Put it in your calendar. Treat play like an important meeting with yourself.
- Start small. You do not need to overhaul your life. Find tiny ways to inject fun into your routine, like a five-minute dance break, a silly challenge, or a spontaneous game night.

2. Reconnect With the Joy of Your Childhood

Remember when fun was your default setting?

- Think back. What did you love to do as a kid? Drawing? Climbing trees? Making up ridiculous stories? Do that.

- Try new things. If you have been wanting to take a painting class, learn an instrument, or attempt roller-skating again, do it. Play is about exploring without worrying about whether you are good at it.

3. Embrace Spontaneity, Because the Best Moments Are Unplanned

Fun does not always need a game plan. Some of the best experiences happen when you throw structure out the window.

- Say yes. If an opportunity for fun pops up, take it. Join the game, jump in the lake, or go on that spontaneous road trip.
- Let go of perfection. Playfulness thrives when you stop worrying about looking ridiculous. Allow yourself to make mistakes, be silly, and laugh at yourself.

4. Turn Everyday Tasks into Play

Life is filled with responsibilities, but that does not mean it has to be dull.

- Gamify tasks. Turn boring chores into a game. Race against the clock while cleaning, make a playlist for errands, or challenge yourself to make something routine more interesting.
- Bring humor into interactions. Send a funny meme to a friend, crack a joke at work, or bring some lightheartedness to your conversations.

5. Create a Playful Environment

Your surroundings can either encourage or stifle fun.

- Add elements of play to your space. Keep things around that make you smile, like colorful artwork, a deck of cards, or even a jar of fun challenges to pull from when you need a break.

- Surround yourself with playful people. If you are always around serious, negative energy, it is going to rub off. Spend time with people who make you laugh, who bring out your fun side, and who remind you to lighten up.

6. Be Fully Present in Play

Play is not just about the activity itself, but about the mindset you bring to it.

- Focus on the moment. When you are engaged in play, let yourself fully enjoy it. Stop checking your phone, stop overthinking, and just be in the experience.
- Savor the joy. Take a moment to recognize how play makes you feel and how it adds richness to your life.

7. Let Go of Inhibitions

The biggest roadblock to playfulness is the voice in your head saying, "I am too old for this" or "I do not have time." That voice is lying.

- Challenge your inner critic. The only thing stopping you from playing is the belief that you should not. Let that go.
- Give yourself permission. Playfulness does not have to be loud or obvious. It can be as simple as a playful thought, a smile, or a joke.

8. Cultivate a Playful Mindset

Play is not just about what you do; it is about how you see the world.

- Adopt a "yes, and" approach. In improv, the rule is to accept what is happening and build on it. Do the same in life.
- Find the humor. Laugh at life's weirdness, at your own mistakes, and at the ridiculousness of it all.

By following these steps, you will gradually infuse more playfulness into your life, making it richer, more joyful, and full of moments that remind you not to take everything so seriously. Play is not just about having fun. It is about feeling *alive.*

Finding Your Playmates: Because Life is Too Short for Boring People

Surrounding yourself with people who encourage your playful spirit is like adding hot sauce to an otherwise bland meal—everything just gets a little more exciting, unpredictable, and full of flavor. The company you keep can either hype you up and amplify your joy or suck the life right out of you like a human vacuum cleaner. So, choose wisely. You need people who make even the simplest moments feel like an adventure, the kind of friends who turn a routine grocery trip into a cart-racing competition or make a mundane Tuesday night feel like a festival.

Think of your playful friends as the secret ingredient that keeps life from feeling like a never-ending to-do list. When you surround yourself with people who actually *enjoy* life, it rubs off on you. Their enthusiasm fuels yours, and before you know it, you are laughing louder, dreaming bigger, and saying yes to things that make life a hell of a lot more fun.

Be intentional about the company you keep. Find the people who encourage you to be unapologetically you, who remind you that play is not a waste of time, and who know that the best memories come from unplanned, ridiculous, laugh-until-you-cry moments. Because when your circle is filled with the kind of people who lift your spirits instead of dragging you down, life becomes a much more thrilling ride.

1. Identify Your Playful Peeps

First things first, figure out who in your life naturally brings out your fun side. These are the people who make you belly laugh, who say yes to random adventures, and who could probably find a way to make waiting at the DMV entertaining. They are the ones who remind you what it feels like to be lighthearted, carefree, and genuinely in the moment.

If you are feeling like your current crew is more "buzzkill" than "buzzing with excitement," it might be time to expand your circle. Find the spaces where playfulness is celebrated—join a dance class, sign up for a game night, or start hanging around people who do not take themselves so damn seriously. You cannot expect to live a fun, adventurous life if you are surrounded by people who treat fun like an inconvenience.

The key here is simple: put yourself in environments that naturally bring out playfulness, and watch as your tribe finds *you*.

2. Create a Positive Feedback Loop of Fun

Once you have found your people, it is time to make fun a regular thing—not just a once-in-a-blue-moon kind of deal. Playfulness should be an *expectation* in your friendships, not an occasional bonus.

Plan experiences that keep the energy alive. Whether it is impromptu karaoke nights, themed dinner parties, roller-skating challenges, or a "who can embarrass themselves the most in public" contest, it does not matter. The point is to make fun a *priority* and not just something that happens when schedules magically align.

Give yourself permission to be ridiculous, to step outside of your comfort zone, and to embrace the kind of joy that is entirely unfiltered. The more you make playfulness a habit, the more it will spill over into other parts of your life. Suddenly, challenges seem less daunting, stress feels more manageable, and the serious stuff gets balanced out by much-needed moments of lightness.

Your playful tribe will become the fuel that keeps you going, lifting you up when things get tough and reminding you that life is not just about surviving—it is about thriving.

3. Cultivate a Playful and Supportive Environment

The best playmates are not just fun—they are the ones who remind you to laugh when life sucker-punches you. Playfulness is not just about goofing off; it is about finding humor even in the roughest moments. The best people to have around are the ones who know how to keep things light without dismissing the serious stuff.

Your ideal circle should include people who not only encourage fun but also have your back when things get heavy. These are the friends who will get you out of your funk with a well-timed joke, who know how to turn stress into something manageable, and who remind you that even in chaos, there is always a reason to laugh.

When you surround yourself with people who know how to balance play and support, you create an environment where joy and resilience go hand in hand. These friendships become your safety net, keeping you from getting lost in the grind and reminding you that life is meant to be *enjoyed*.

Playful, supportive friendships are the game-changer you never knew you needed. Find them, nurture them, and hold onto them tight.

Journaling Prompts: Unleashing Your Inner Child

Before diving into these prompts, let's take a second to remember that play is *not* just some optional, once-in-a-while indulgence. It is part of being a happy, well-rounded human. These questions are here to help you tap into that playful energy, giving you clarity on how to bring more fun into your life. Grab a journal, drop the self-judgment, and let's get into it.

- **Reflect on Your Playful Self**

  When was the last time you felt truly playful and free? Describe that moment. What were you doing, who were you with, and how did it make you feel?

- **Rediscover Childhood Joys**

  Think back to your childhood. What activities or games did you love? How can you bring those things back into your life now?

- **Find Your Playful Tribe**

  Who in your life brings out your fun side? How can you spend more time with them or build new relationships that encourage playfulness?

- **Overcoming Barriers to Play**

  What stops you from being more playful? What beliefs or fears hold you back? How can you let go of them?

- **Plan a Playful Adventure**

  If you had an entire day dedicated to play, how would you spend it? Write out your dream "play day" and figure out how to make it happen.

- **Playfulness in Everyday Life**

  What are some simple ways you can make your daily routine more fun and lighthearted?

- **The Role of Humor**

  How often do you laugh each day? What makes you laugh the most? How can you invite more humor into your life?

- **Embracing Playfulness in Relationships**

  How do you express playfulness in your relationships? What impact does it have, and how can you bring more of it into your connections?

- **Exploring New Playful Pursuits**

  Is there a hobby or activity you have been curious about but have not tried yet? What is holding you back? What is one step you can take toward trying it?

- **Playfulness as a Path to Growth**

  Think about a time when being playful helped you through a challenge. How did it shift your perspective?

Play is Not Optional—It is Necessary

As we close out this chapter, let's get one thing straight. Play is *not* a luxury. It is not something you will get around to "when you have time." It is a lifeline. It is the thing that keeps life from feeling like a never-ending grind.

Play nurtures creativity. It strengthens relationships. It makes even the hardest days a little more bearable. And when you embrace play, you are not just making your own life better—you are inspiring others to do the same.

So, as you move forward, make play a non-negotiable part of your life. Whether it is through a hobby, time with friends, or simply finding humor in the absurdity of life, let yourself *enjoy* the ride.

Because at the end of the day, the most meaningful moments are not the ones spent grinding yourself into exhaustion. They are the ones where you let go, laugh, and remember that life is meant to be *lived*.

Chapter 10

The Art of Letting Go

"The art of letting go is not about losing. It is about making space for what truly belongs in your life, allowing freedom and peace to fill the voids once held by resistance." —Jamie

The Art of Letting Go: Clearing Out the Emotional Clutter

Letting go is not just about releasing a bad habit or walking away from a toxic relationship. It is about making a conscious decision to stop gripping onto things that no longer serve you—no matter how familiar, comfortable, or ingrained they may be. It is about recognizing when something is keeping you stuck in a cycle that you have outgrown and having the courage to break free.

And let me tell you, nothing teaches you about the brutal yet beautiful art of letting go like getting sober.

Letting Go to Save Myself

When I decided to get sober, I did not just have to let go of alcohol and cocaine. I had to let go of the entire identity I had built around them. I had to step away from the people I once considered my closest friends, the ones I had partied with, shared highs with, and convinced myself would always be in my life. At the time, it felt like I was losing everything. But in reality, I was finally choosing *me.*

Addiction thrives in certain environments and so does healing. I learned quickly that I could not keep one foot in my old world and one foot in the new one. If I was serious about staying clean, I had to stop surrounding myself with people who still lived for the next party, the next high, or the next round of shots.

There were friends I truly cared about, but every time I was around them, it was like stepping back into my old life. The memories, the habits, the temptations—it was all there, waiting for me. And as much as I wanted to believe I was strong enough to be around it without slipping, I had to be honest with myself. If I wanted to change, I had to change *everything*, starting with the people I surrounded myself with.

It was one of the hardest things I have ever done. There is a loneliness that comes with letting go of the people who once felt like home. But I had to ask myself, *Was it really home? Or was it just familiar?* Because there is a big difference.

True friendship should uplift you, not pull you back into the darkness you fought so hard to escape. And when I started letting go, I realized something powerful—those people were never really my friends. They were my *co-conspirators* in self-destruction. They did not want me to get better because it forced them to look at their own demons. When I stopped drinking and using, it made them uncomfortable. It made them realize that they were still trapped in a cycle I had decided to leave.

And so, I let them go. Not out of anger, not because I did not care about them, but because I finally cared about *me* more.

The Weight of What We Hold Onto

Holding onto the past, negative emotions, or unmet expectations is like dragging a suitcase full of bricks everywhere you go and wondering why you feel exhausted all the time. At some point, you must put the damn thing down.

- The past happened. You cannot rewrite it, but you can stop letting it define your present. Staying attached to it keeps you stuck in a chapter that has already been written.
- Negative emotions like anger, resentment, or guilt can teach us lessons, but they should not become our permanent address. Holding onto them only means we are choosing to suffer over and over again.
- Unfulfilled expectations are a sneaky weight to carry. We all have an idea of how life was *supposed* to go. The dream job, the perfect relationship, the flawless version of ourselves. When reality does not match up, we can either drown in disappointment or accept that maybe life has something even better planned.

Letting go is not just about removing something from your life. It is about making space for something new. And if your hands are full of the past, you will never be able to reach for the future.

Why Letting Go is Essential for Growth

Letting go is not a one-time event. It is a practice. It is a commitment to yourself, a vow that you will not hold onto anything that drags you down just because it is hard to say goodbye.

Here is why it is so damn necessary.

It creates space for better things. When your hands are full of the past, you cannot grab onto the future. Imagine trying to carry a brand-new opportunity while still gripping onto the people, habits, or pain that no longer serve you. It does not work.

It stops the cycle of suffering. How many times have you replayed a painful memory, expecting the ending to somehow change? It never does. The only way to end the suffering is to step out of the cycle.

It frees you from what is not yours to carry. Some things were never yours to hold onto in the first place. Other people's opinions, their mistakes, their choices. Letting go means understanding what is yours to heal and what is not your responsibility.

It realigns you with your soul's purpose. If you are holding onto something just because it is familiar, you are probably blocking yourself from something that is actually meant for you.

Letting Go in Action. How to Actually Do It

So, how do you let go of things that feel like they are a part of you? You take it step by step.

Accept That It's Time

The first and hardest step is accepting that something has run its course. Whether it is a belief, a relationship, or a personal narrative, acknowledge that it is no longer serving your highest good.

Let Yourself Feel It

Letting go does not mean numbing out. Feel the grief, the discomfort, the sadness. Sit with it. Let it move through you instead of pushing it down or pretending it does not exist.

Rewrite the Story

Instead of seeing it as a loss, see it as a redirection. Instead of thinking you failed, shift to seeing that you learned. Instead of believing you lost something important, reframe it as making space for something better.

Stop Replaying What You Cannot Change

Replaying old conversations, missed opportunities, and past hurts is like picking at a scab and wondering why it never heals. Catch yourself in the act and redirect your thoughts.

Focus on the Present

The best way to move forward is to root yourself in the now. Practice gratitude, engage in things that bring you joy, and immerse yourself in experiences that remind you life is still happening right now.

Trust That What's Meant for You Will Stay

The things, people, and opportunities that are truly meant for you will not require you to hold on so tightly. What is aligned with you will flow naturally.

New Sneakers and Fresh Starts

Letting go is kind of like throwing away your favorite pair of worn-out sneakers. They are scuffed up, they do not fit like they used to, and honestly, they probably smell a little funky. But you have had them for so long that it feels wrong to toss them.

Still, if you never clear out the old, there is no room for the new. Holding onto what is familiar might feel safe, but it keeps you from stepping into something better. Life is not meant to be a never-ending loop of the same stories. It is meant to evolve.

So, if something in your life is screaming for release. If a relationship, a habit, or a past hurt is holding you hostage. Maybe it is time to let it go. Maybe it is time to stop gripping so tightly and trust that what is ahead is so much better than what you are leaving behind.

Let go. Make space. And get ready to step into the next chapter of your life, fresh sneakers and all.

Understanding What Letting Go Really Means

Letting go is one of those phrases that gets thrown around like a self-help buzzword. People say it all the time. *Just let it go. Move on. Release it.*

Sounds easy, right? But if you have ever tried to actually do it, you know that letting go can feel more like trying to untangle a necklace chain that has been sitting in a jewelry box for a decade. It is messy, frustrating, and sometimes it feels damn near impossible.

Letting go is not about shrugging your shoulders and giving up. It is not about pretending something did not matter or acting like the past never happened. It is not about erasing parts of your story. It is about deciding that those parts no longer get to define you. It is about freeing yourself from the weight of what no longer serves you so that you can finally move forward without dragging the past behind you like a broken suitcase with one wheel barely hanging on.

At its core, letting go is an act of power. It is reclaiming your energy and choosing where to direct it. It is understanding that not everything and everyone deserves space in your mind, your heart, or your life. It is about making peace with the fact that some things did not turn out the way you wanted them to, some people were not who you thought they were, and some chapters needed to end so that better ones could begin.

Letting Go is Not Losing Control—It is Gaining Freedom

One of the biggest misconceptions about letting go is that it means losing control. But here is the truth. You never had control in the first place. Life is unpredictable. People will make their own choices. Circumstances will change whether you like it or not. Holding on too tightly to how you think things *should* be only creates stress, resistance, and frustration.

Letting go is about surrendering the illusion of control and choosing to trust instead. Trust that things will unfold the way they are meant to. Trust that even if something does not go your way, you will still be okay.

Trust that the universe, or whatever you believe in, is not out to get you but is actually guiding you toward something better.

This does not mean you sit back and do nothing. It does not mean you stop trying. It means you stop gripping so tightly to things that are outside of your control and start focusing on what *is* within your power—your choices, your mindset, and how you respond to life's curveballs.

Letting go does not make you passive. It makes you adaptable. It means you stop banging on doors that are closed and start looking for the ones that are open.

Not Everything Deserves a Spot in Your Carry-On

We all have emotional baggage. Some of it is necessary. The lessons we have learned, the experiences that have shaped us, the memories that remind us who we are. But not everything deserves a permanent place in our carry-on.

Some things need to be unpacked and left behind.

The toxic friendships that drain you more than they support you.

The old mistakes that keep whispering in your ear, telling you that you are not good enough.

The relationships that ended, but you still replay in your mind like a song stuck on repeat.

The expectations that life *had* to go a certain way or else it was not worth living.

Letting go means looking at everything you are carrying and asking yourself, *Does this help me, or does this hold me back?* If it is the latter, it is time to release it.

This is not about forgetting or pretending things did not happen. It is about choosing what gets to come with you into your next chapter.

Letting Go is Self-Love in Action

Choosing to let go is one of the most radical acts of self-love you can commit to. It is saying, I refuse to let my past define my future. I refuse to let pain, resentment, or disappointment dictate my happiness. I refuse to hold onto anything that costs me my peace.

It takes courage to do this. It takes patience. Some things take time to release, and that is okay. You do not have to wake up one morning and suddenly feel completely free of everything that has ever hurt you. But with every conscious choice to let go, you get a little lighter. A little freer. A little more at peace with where you are and where you are going.

Letting go is not a one-time event. It is a practice. It is something you will have to do again and again. But each time, it will get a little easier. And each time, you will remind yourself that your life is not meant to be weighed down by the things you were never meant to carry.

Because at the end of the day, letting go is not about losing. It is about making space for something better.

Clarifying Misconceptions. Letting Go is Not Giving Up. It is Making Space for Something Better

One of the biggest lies people tell themselves about letting go is that it means giving up. Like you are admitting failure. Like you were not strong enough to make something work. That kind of thinking is complete nonsense.

Letting go is not quitting. It is not backing down. It is not you throwing in the towel because you could not handle the challenge. Letting go is a conscious choice to stop holding onto something that is no longer meant for you. It is about knowing when a chapter has ended, when a person no longer belongs in your life, when an old version of yourself needs to be shed so you can grow.

It is about power. It is about reclaiming your energy and choosing where to direct it. Because holding onto things that drain you, break you down, or keep you in cycles of pain is not strength. It is self-sabotage.

So, let's be real. Letting go is not about losing. It is about making space. It is about clearing out what no longer fits in your life so you can receive something better. It is about making peace with what was, accepting what is, and opening yourself up to what could be.

If you are gripping onto something with all your might, your hands are too full to catch something new. Letting go is about opening your hands, your mind, and your heart so that when something better comes along, you are actually able to receive it.

And before you start thinking that letting go is something you do once and never have to deal with again, let me stop you right there. Letting go is a practice. It is something you will have to do over and over again, with different people, different situations, different versions of yourself. And each time you do it, you are making room for something greater.

So no, letting go is not giving up. It is choosing yourself. And that is the most powerful thing you can do.

Letting Go is Not the Same as Suppression. Why You Need to Face It Before You Can Release It

Let's get something straight. Letting go does not mean pretending something did not happen. It does not mean pushing your emotions down so deep that you hope they just disappear on their own. That is called suppression. And suppression is the emotional equivalent of shoving everything into a closet and hoping it never bursts open. Spoiler alert. It always bursts open.

Shoving down your emotions might feel like a quick fix, but it is like trying to hold a beach ball underwater. It will pop back up, probably at the worst possible moment. Suppressed emotions do not just go away. They fester. They morph into resentment, bitterness, stress, anxiety, and even physical illness. They seep into your relationships, your confidence, and your ability to move forward.

Letting go, on the other hand, is an active process. It means you face whatever is weighing you down, sit with it, acknowledge it, and then consciously choose to release it. It requires honesty. You cannot let go of something if you are still in denial that it is affecting you.

The difference between letting go and suppression is the difference between healing and just slapping a bandage over a deep wound. Suppression covers up the issue, but the wound remains. Letting go means you actually take the time to clean it out, no matter how painful it might be, so it can finally heal.

If you want to truly let go, you have to do the work. That means allowing yourself to feel the discomfort instead of running from it. It means sitting with your emotions, processing them, and then choosing to move forward. Letting go is about healing, not hiding.

How to Know When It is Time to Let Go

Sometimes, we hold onto things for so long that we do not even realize they are weighing us down. It becomes second nature to carry pain, resentment, or old versions of ourselves as if they are permanent parts of who we are. But they are not. And when something is no longer serving you, there are always signs. You just have to be willing to recognize them.

1. You Are Constantly Stressed or Anxious

If something in your life is draining you more than it is fueling you, that is a sign. If a relationship, job, habit, or situation makes you feel exhausted rather than energized, it is time to ask yourself why you are still holding on.

2. You Feel More Resentment Than Joy

Resentment is a clear sign that something is not right. If you find yourself feeling bitter toward someone, if you are replaying old arguments in your head, or if you are stuck in a cycle of anger, you need to ask yourself what is keeping you there.

3. It Feels Like You Are Forcing It

Not everything is meant to be forced. If you are constantly bending over backward trying to make something work, if you are the only one putting in effort, or if you are holding onto something out of fear rather than love, it is worth questioning whether it is truly meant for you.

4. Your Gut is Telling You to Move On

Your intuition always knows. You might try to ignore it. You might try to logic your way around it. But deep down, you know when something is not right anymore. That feeling in your gut that keeps nagging at you? Listen to it.

5. You Have Stopped Growing

If you feel stuck, uninspired, or like you are just going through the motions, that is a sign something needs to change. Growth requires change. If you are clinging to something that is keeping you stagnant, you are holding yourself back.

Letting go is not easy. It is uncomfortable. It forces you to step into the unknown. But the alternative is staying stuck. And honestly, that is a hell of a lot scarier than stepping forward into something new.

Common Areas Where We Struggle to Let Go

Some things are harder to release than others. The things we struggle with the most usually have deep emotional ties, making them feel like they are part of us. But they are not. Recognizing what is hardest to let go of can be the first step in finally freeing yourself.

Toxic Relationships

We hold onto people longer than we should. Out of guilt. Out of fear of being alone. Out of habit. But staying in a relationship that drains you, whether it is romantic, friendship, or family, does nothing but keep you stuck in cycles of pain. Letting go does not mean you do not care. It means you care about yourself enough to walk away.

Past Hurts and Regrets

We replay old mistakes, relive past heartbreaks, and beat ourselves up for things we cannot change. But holding onto past pain only ensures you keep suffering from it. It happened. It taught you something. Now let it go.

Expectations and Perfectionism

Life does not always go according to plan. Holding onto rigid expectations keeps you stuck in a cycle of disappointment. The sooner you let go of how you think things *should* be, the sooner you can start embracing how things *actually are* and finding joy in that.

Material Things That No Longer Serve You

We attach emotions to objects. That old sweater from your ex. The stacks of books you swear you will read but never will. The clutter that fills your space and your mind. Letting go of physical things can be just as freeing as releasing emotional baggage.

The Emotional Process of Letting Go

Letting go is not just a mental decision. It is an emotional process that requires time, patience, and self-compassion. It is about facing what has been holding you back, processing it, and then consciously choosing to release it.

So, whatever it is you are holding onto, ask yourself. Is this helping me, or is this holding me back? If it is not adding to your life, it is subtracting from it. And that means it is time to let it go.

The Stages of Emotional Letting Go. Recognition, Acceptance, Release, and Renewal

Letting go is not a quick decision. It is not something you wake up one day and magically accomplish before moving on with your life like nothing ever happened. If only it were that easy. No, letting go is a process. It unfolds in stages, and each one serves a purpose in getting you to a place where you are no longer carrying the emotional baggage that has been weighing you down.

Think of it like a four-course meal—each stage offering up something different. Some parts are tough to swallow, some are surprisingly satisfying, and by the end, you feel lighter, freer, and ready for whatever comes next.

Recognition. The Moment You Know Something Has to Change

This is the "Oh, hell no" moment. The realization that whatever you are holding onto—whether it is a relationship, a past mistake, an expectation, or an outdated version of yourself—is no longer serving you. This is where you stop making excuses. You stop justifying why you are still holding on. You stop pretending everything is fine when it is clearly not.

Recognition can hit you like a ton of bricks or creep up slowly over time. Maybe it is waking up one morning and realizing you have been putting all your energy into something that does not even make you happy anymore. Maybe it is hearing that little voice in your head whisper, *You deserve better*, and finally believing it. Maybe it is looking in the mirror and realizing you have been shrinking yourself to fit into spaces you have long outgrown.

Whatever the case, this is the moment you acknowledge that something needs to change. That you cannot keep gripping onto something that is only bringing you stress, pain, or stagnation. That this thing you have been carrying is way too heavy, and it is about damn time you put it down.

Acceptance. Facing Reality Without Fighting It

This is where things start to get uncomfortable, because now you are not just recognizing the need for change—you are sitting with it. Acceptance is about facing reality without sugarcoating it, without wishing things had turned out differently, and without trying to bend the past to fit your expectations.

This does not mean you suddenly become okay with everything. It does not mean you ignore your emotions or pretend you are fine when you are not. It means you stop resisting what is. You stop arguing with reality. You stop thinking, *If only things had gone this way instead...* because they didn't, and no amount of wishing can rewrite the past.

This is also where you start releasing blame—whether it is toward yourself, another person, or the universe itself. Maybe you made mistakes. Maybe someone hurt you. Maybe life threw a curveball you never saw coming. Either way, acceptance means choosing to move forward instead of replaying what went wrong over and over again in your head.

It is about shifting from Why did this happen to me? to, What can I learn from this?

It is the moment you say, This is where I am. This is what happened. And I am choosing to move forward anyway.

Release Letting Go Instead of Just Talking About It

Now comes the real work. The part where you stop just thinking about letting go and actually do it.

This is where you release the grip you have had on whatever has been holding you back. Whether it is physically removing something from your life, setting a boundary, changing a belief, or even just shifting your perspective, this stage is all about taking action.

This could mean:

Writing a letter, you will never send, pouring out everything you need to say, and then burning it or tearing it up.

Deleting old texts, photos, and reminders that keep you stuck in the past. Blocking the number of that person you know you need to stop giving access to your energy.
Dropping the self-imposed guilt that has been making you feel unworthy.

Finally putting an end to the overthinking, the what-ifs, and the "maybe one day" fantasies about something that is never going to happen.

Release is the moment you decide, *I am done carrying this.* And let me tell you, when you truly release something, when you stop letting it take up space in your heart, your mind, and your life, the freedom you feel is nothing short of life-changing.

Renewal, The Fresh Start You Did Not Know You Needed

This is the reward for all the hard work. Renewal is the feeling of walking into a space that has been completely decluttered. It is breathing easier. It is feeling lighter. It is no longer being triggered by something that once consumed you.

It is waking up and realizing you no longer think about that thing, that person, that past version of yourself as much as you used to. It is finally making room for what is meant for you instead of staying stuck in what was.

Renewal does not mean forgetting. It does not mean everything is perfect. It means you have finally freed yourself from whatever was holding you back. It means you can look forward without constantly glancing over your shoulder.

It is stepping into the next chapter of your life with open hands instead of clenched fists.

The Process of Letting Go is Not Always Linear

One important thing to remember? You do not just go through these stages once and then magically have everything figured out. Letting go is not always a straight path. Some days, you will feel completely free, and then out of nowhere, a memory, a song, or a random thought will pull you back in. That does not mean you are failing. It just means you are human.

Healing happens in layers. Sometimes, you will need to go through the process of recognition, acceptance, release, and renewal more than once before something fully lets go of *you.* That is normal.

What matters is that you keep moving forward. That you do not let yourself stay stuck in something that was never meant to be permanent. That you keep choosing yourself over and over again.

Because when you do, you will realize that letting go is not the end of the story—it is the beginning of something so much better.

How to Cope with the Discomfort of Change and Uncertainty

Letting go sounds great in theory, right? Release the past, embrace the new, step into your power, all that good stuff. But in reality, letting go often feels like jumping out of a plane and hoping you do not end up as a human pancake. The discomfort of change and uncertainty is real. It is that pit-in-your-stomach, "What the hell am I doing?" feeling that makes you want to run right back to what is familiar, even if what is familiar is complete garbage.

But here is the thing—discomfort is part of the process. Growth does not happen in your comfort zone. And learning how to sit with that discomfort, instead of trying to escape it, is what separates the people who evolve from the ones who stay stuck. So, how do you deal with it without losing your mind? Here are some tried-and-true methods for getting through the awkward, messy, gut-wrenching middle part of transformation.

1. Embrace Mindfulness. Stop Fighting the Present Moment

Think of mindfulness as your mental safety harness. It keeps you from spiraling out of control when everything around you feels unstable. The key to navigating uncertainty is not trying to predict the future or control every outcome—it is about staying present and reminding yourself that right now, in this moment, you are okay.

Start small. The next time you feel overwhelmed by change, pause and take a deep breath. Notice what is happening around you. Listen to the sounds in the room. Feel the ground beneath your feet. The goal is to bring yourself back into the here and now instead of letting your mind race ten steps ahead to every worst-case scenario imaginable.

Uncertainty becomes a lot less terrifying when you stop trying to control everything and instead focus on what is actually happening in the moment. You cannot predict the future, but you *can* handle what is right in front of you.

2. Lean on Your Support System. Find Your Hype Squad

You do not have to go through this alone. Seriously, if you are trying to navigate massive life changes without a support system, you are making things way harder than they need to be. Find your people—the ones who will listen when you need to vent, remind you why you started this journey, and maybe even throw snacks at you when you are being dramatic.

Your support system does not have to be huge. It could be a best friend, a family member, a therapist, or even your dog (because let's be real, dogs give excellent emotional support). The point is to have people in your corner who remind you that you are not crazy for choosing growth over stagnation.

And do not be afraid to *ask* for support. If you need reassurance, ask for it. If you need someone to tell you you are making the right decision, say so. You are not weak for needing help—you are human.

3. Practice Self-Compassion. Let Yourself Be a Messy Work in Progress

Letting go is not an overnight success story. It is not a straight line. It is a rollercoaster, complete with emotional loop-de-loops and unexpected drops. Some days, you will feel like you have got it all figured out. Other days, you will want to crawl into bed and pretend the world does not exist.

That is normal. And beating yourself up for struggling only makes it worse.

Give yourself permission to be imperfect. Give yourself credit for every small step forward. Change is hard enough without adding self-judgment into the mix. Speak to yourself the way you would a close friend—because I promise, you would never be as harsh on them as you are on yourself.

4. Focus on What You Can Control. Stop Trying to Wrestle the Universe

Nothing will drive you crazier than trying to control things that are completely out of your hands. The truth is, most things in life are uncertain. People change. Plans fall apart. Life throws curveballs. And fighting against that reality is a one-way ticket to exhaustion and frustration.

Instead of obsessing over the unknown, shift your focus to what *is* within your control. You may not be able to predict the future, but you *can* control how you show up today. You can control your mindset, your actions, and how you respond to challenges.

If everything feels overwhelming, break it down into small, manageable tasks. Take control of the things that ground you—your morning routine, what you eat, what time you go to bed. Even little decisions, like choosing what music to listen to or what book to read, can help you feel a sense of stability when everything else feels chaotic.

The unknown is scary. But you are still in charge of *you*.

Techniques for Letting Go. How to Actually Do It Instead of Just Thinking About It

So, you have decided it is time to let go. You are ready to drop the emotional dead weight. But how do you actually *do* it? Because let's be real, saying "I am letting go" is one thing. Actually feeling like you have released something is another.

Here are some practical ways to help your mind and heart catch up to your decision.

Mindfulness Practices. Bring Awareness to What Needs to Be Released

You cannot let go of something if you are not even fully aware that you are holding onto it. Mindfulness helps you tune in to what is going on internally—what beliefs, memories, or emotions are still lingering beneath the surface.

Try sitting in stillness for a few minutes and just observing your thoughts. What keeps coming up? What emotions are attached to those thoughts? Are there any patterns you notice? This simple awareness can be the first step in truly letting go.

Visualization Exercises. See Yourself Letting Go

Your brain is a powerful tool. When you visualize yourself releasing something, your mind starts to accept it as reality.

Picture yourself dropping a heavy bag you have been carrying. Imagine the relief in your body. Or visualize tying your emotional baggage to a balloon and watching it float away. The more vividly you imagine it, the more real it will feel.

Rituals of Release. Do Something Symbolic

Sometimes, physically doing something to represent letting go makes all the difference.

- **Write a letter** to the person, situation, or version of yourself you are releasing. Say everything you need to say. Then burn it, tear it up, or throw it in water.
- **Create a ritual.** Light a candle, say out loud what you are releasing, and then blow it out. Let the flame symbolize the past, and the extinguishing of it marks the beginning of a fresh start.
- **Get rid of objects tied to old energy.** If there is something in your space that keeps you stuck in the past, donate it, throw it away, or repurpose it.

These rituals help signal to your subconscious mind that it is time to move forward.

Breathwork and Meditation. Clear the Emotional Clutter

Breathwork is an underrated but powerful tool for letting go. When emotions get stuck in your body, deep, intentional breathing can help move that energy through and out.

Try this simple exercise:

- Breathe in deeply, hold for a few seconds, and imagine yourself gathering up everything you are ready to release.
- Breathe out slowly and picture it all leaving your body.

Repeat until you feel lighter.

Final Thoughts. Letting Go is a Gift to Yourself

Letting go is not about forgetting. It is not about pretending something did not matter. It is about freeing yourself from the weight of what no longer serves you so that you can make space for something better.

Will it be uncomfortable? Yes. Will there be days when you want to go back to what is familiar? Absolutely. But every time you choose to release something that is holding you back, you are choosing *you*.

And if that is not the ultimate act of self-love, I do not know what is.

How to Forgive Yourself and Others. Letting Go of Guilt and Resentment Without Losing Your Mind

Forgiveness is one of those things that sounds nice in theory but feels damn near impossible when you are actually in the thick of it. Whether it is forgiving someone else for screwing you over or forgiving yourself for past mistakes, the struggle is real. But here is the thing—holding onto resentment and guilt is like drinking poison and expecting someone else to feel sick. The only person you are hurting is you.

So, let's get into it. How do you actually forgive, without feeling like you are just letting people (or yourself) off the hook?

Step 1. Acknowledge the Hurt Instead of Pretending It Did Not Happen

Before you can forgive, you need to face the wound head-on. None of this *"It wasn't that bad"* or *"I should just get over it"* nonsense. If something hurt you, it hurt you. Period.

Acknowledge what happened and how it made you feel. Whether it was betrayal, disappointment, or a mistake that left you drowning in guilt, recognize it for what it is. You cannot heal what you refuse to look at.

And if it is yourself you are forgiving? Stop acting like you are the only person on the planet who has ever messed up. Newsflash. We all have.

Step 2. Try to Understand the Why (Without Making Excuses)

Understanding does not mean excusing, but it *does* help you put things into perspective. People hurt others for a variety of reasons—sometimes out of their own pain, sometimes out of ignorance, sometimes because they are just selfish jerks. And guess what? Sometimes *you* were the one acting out of fear, insecurity, or straight-up bad judgment.

Take a step back and ask yourself.

- **Was this intentional?**
- **Was this person operating from a place of their own wounds?**
- **Was I doing the best I could with what I knew at the time?**

Understanding why something happened does not mean it is okay. But it does help you see that holding onto resentment, guilt, or anger is only keeping *you* stuck.

Step 3. Make the Decision to Forgive (Even If You Are Not Totally Ready Yet)

Here is the truth—waiting until you *feel* like forgiving is a trap. You might never wake up one morning and think, *Wow, today feels like a great day to forgive that person who royally screwed me over.*

Forgiveness is not a feeling. It is a choice. A conscious decision to stop letting the past hold power over you. It does not mean you excuse what happened, nor does it mean you have to welcome someone back into your life with open arms. It just means you are ready to release the grip this situation has on your emotions.

And if you are forgiving yourself? It means choosing to move forward instead of punishing yourself indefinitely for something you cannot change.

Step 4. Express the Forgiveness (Even If the Other Person Never Knows About It)

Forgiveness does not require a big dramatic reconciliation moment. You do not need to call up the person who hurt you and give them a heartfelt speech about how you are finally letting it go. In fact, sometimes the best thing you can do is keep that energy to yourself.

Write a letter you never send. Say the words out loud to yourself. Hell, scream it into a pillow if you need to. The act of expressing forgiveness—whether to another person or yourself—helps solidify it in your mind.

And if someone is *truly* sorry? You get to decide whether they deserve a second chance in your life. Forgiveness is not the same as trust. Forgiveness is free. Trust is earned.

Step 5. Let Go of the Guilt and Resentment Instead of Letting It Eat You Alive

Resentment is like carrying a backpack full of bricks. Every day, it weighs you down a little more. And guilt? That is just self-inflicted torture disguised as a moral compass.

Neither of these things are helping you.

If you are forgiving yourself, it is time to stop beating yourself up. Holding onto guilt does not make you a better person—it just keeps you stuck in shame, and shame keeps you from growing. If you are forgiving someone else, it is time to let go of the resentment that has been living rent-free in your mind.

Release it. Burn the letter. Cut the cord. Take the damn backpack off.

Step 6. Shift Your Focus to the Future Instead of Wasting Energy on the Past

After forgiveness comes freedom. This is your chance to take all that energy you were spending on anger, blame, or guilt and put it toward something that actually *benefits* you. Growth. Healing. New opportunities. A fresh start.

The past is done. You cannot change it. But you *can* change how you carry it moving forward.

The Connection Between Forgiveness and Inner Peace. Why Holding a Grudge is Only Hurting You

There is a direct line between forgiveness and peace of mind. When you hold onto anger, resentment, or guilt, you are the one carrying the weight. Not the other person. *You.*

Think of it like this. If you were carrying around a giant rock everywhere you went, would it make your life easier or harder? Exactly. So why are you carrying around emotional weights that serve no purpose?

Forgiving someone is not about letting them off the hook. It is about taking back your *own* peace. It is about refusing to let the past steal any more of your joy.

When you forgive, you are not just doing it for them—you are doing it for you.

Embracing the Freedom of Letting Go. Why This is the Ultimate Power Move

Forgiveness is not weakness. Letting go is not surrender. It is actually the most badass thing you can do.

When you release grudges, regrets, and guilt, you are setting yourself free. You are reclaiming your energy. You are refusing to let pain dictate your future.

And the best part? The second you stop carrying all that emotional baggage, you create space for better things. New experiences. Deeper relationships. Inner peace.

Letting go is not about losing. It is about *winning*—winning back your joy, your clarity, and your ability to move forward without the weight of the past dragging behind you.

Final Thoughts. The Choice is Yours

Forgiveness is a gift you give yourself. It is not about whether someone *deserves* it. It is about whether *you* deserve peace.

So, do you want to keep carrying around resentment, anger, and guilt like some kind of emotional hoarder? Or do you want to drop the weight, take a deep breath, and finally move the hell on?

The choice is yours.

Living a Life of Detachment and Flow. Letting Go Without Losing Yourself

Imagine gliding through life like a leaf floating down a stream, effortlessly moving with the current rather than getting snagged on every damn rock and twig along the way. That is what it means to live with detachment and flow—finding that sweet spot between caring deeply and clinging desperately. It is about showing up, doing your best, and then surrendering the outcome instead of white-knuckling your way through life trying to control everything.

This is not about being indifferent. It is not about throwing your hands up and saying, *"Whatever, I do not care."* Detachment is about holding things lightly rather than gripping them so hard that they break under pressure. It is about knowing what you want, taking action toward it, and then trusting that whatever unfolds is meant for you. It is about recognizing that life is a constantly shifting, ever-moving experience, and the more you fight against its natural flow, the more exhausted and frustrated you become.

So how do you live in this state of detachment and flow without feeling like you are just passively floating through life, letting everything happen to you? Let's break it down.

The Art of Surrender. Why Clinging Only Creates Suffering

Control is an illusion, but that does not stop most of us from trying to hold onto it with an iron grip. We cling to relationships that are long past their expiration date. We obsess over outcomes, convinced that things *have* to go a certain way for us to be happy. We resist change like a toddler throwing a tantrum, even when it is obvious that change is exactly what we need.

And what does all that clinging get us? Stress. Anxiety. A tight chest and a racing mind.

Surrendering does not mean giving up. It does not mean you stop caring. It means you stop **forcing.** You stop exhausting yourself trying to control the uncontrollable. You start trusting that life has a way of working itself out, often in ways better than you could have imagined.

This does not mean you sit around waiting for miracles to drop into your lap. You still show up. You still do the work. But you also recognize that **your peace does not depend on everything going exactly how you planned.** You allow things to unfold naturally, rather than trying to strong-arm the universe into submission.

Detachment is Not Indifference. It is Emotional Freedom

A lot of people hear the word *detachment* and assume it means not caring. But that could not be further from the truth. Detachment is not about closing yourself off from life—it is about engaging with it fully *without letting it consume you.*

It means loving without possession.

It means striving without desperation.

It means being passionate without being obsessive.

Detachment is the ability to experience life deeply without losing yourself in it. To enjoy relationships, experiences, and achievements without needing them to define you.

Think of it like this. If you are holding onto something too tightly—whether it is a relationship, a job, or an expectation—you suffocate it. You drain the joy out of it. You make it fragile, because its existence becomes tied to your sense of security. But when you hold it with an open hand, you give it room to breathe, to evolve, to be what it is meant to be instead of what you are forcing it to be.

Flow. Letting Life Unfold Instead of Fighting Against It

When you are in flow, life does not feel like an uphill battle. It does not mean everything is always easy, but it does mean you are not constantly swimming against the current.

Flow happens when you trust yourself enough to stop overanalyzing every decision. It happens when you listen to your intuition instead of drowning it out with fear-based thinking. It happens when you embrace change instead of fighting it tooth and nail.

Here is how to cultivate more flow in your life.

1. Stop Overthinking Every Damn Thing

Overthinking is the killer of flow. It is what keeps you stuck, second-guessing every move, afraid of making a wrong turn. But here is the truth—there are no wrong turns. Every decision, every experience, every so-called "mistake" is just a detour leading you to where you are meant to be.

So, take the pressure off. Make a decision and trust yourself. You will figure it out as you go.

2. Listen to Your Gut Instead of Your Fear

Your intuition knows what is best for you, but most of the time, it gets drowned out by fear, doubt, and outside opinions. Flow happens when you learn to recognize the difference.

Fear sounds loud, urgent, and panicked. "What if this goes wrong?" "What if I regret this?"

Intuition is quieter, calmer, and more certain. *"This just feels right."*

Trust that feeling. Follow what excites you. It is leading you somewhere for a reason.

3. Be Present Instead of Always Chasing the Next Thing

When you are constantly fixated on what is next—whether it is the next goal, the next relationship, the next big life event—you miss what is happening *right now.*

Flow means appreciating where you are, even as you work toward where you are going. It is finding joy in the process, not just the outcome. Because here is the truth—if you do not learn how to enjoy the *journey*, you are never going to be satisfied, no matter how much you achieve.

4. Let Go of the Timeline in Your Head

One of the biggest blocks to flow is the belief that things *should* be happening faster. That you *should* be further along by now. That your life *should* look different.

Says who?

There is no universal deadline for success, happiness, or personal growth. Life is unfolding exactly as it should, even if it does not feel that way in the moment. Trust the timing of your life instead of constantly feeling like you are behind.

How Detachment and Flow Create a Life of Freedom

When you master detachment and flow, everything changes. You stop forcing relationships to work that are not meant for you. You stop stressing over things you cannot control. You stop wasting energy on what other people think.

Instead, you start *living*.

You wake up feeling lighter, because you are not carrying the weight of unnecessary expectations. You move through life with more ease, because you are not trying to control every damn thing. You attract better opportunities, better people, and better experiences, because your energy is no longer rooted in desperation or fear.

You finally understand that *you* are not in control of everything—and that is a good thing. Because when you stop micromanaging the universe, you allow it to do what it does best. Work its magic.

Final Thoughts. The Art of Letting Life Be

Living with detachment and flow does not mean life stops being messy. It does not mean you will never face challenges or disappointments. What it does mean is that you will stop making yourself suffer unnecessarily.

It means you will move through life with more peace and less resistance.

It means you will trust that what is meant for you will find you.

It means you will release the pressure and start enjoying the ride.

So, take a deep breath. Let go of the need to control every detail. And remind yourself that *life is meant to be lived, not micromanaged.*

Yes, there is some repetition between this section and the previous one, particularly in the themes of detachment, flow, surrender, and trusting the process. However, I can refine and expand on this section to eliminate unnecessary overlap while still keeping the essence intact. Here's a refreshed version with the same message but a fresh approach:

Practicing Non-Attachment in Daily Life. Caring Without Clinging

Non-attachment is not about becoming an emotionless robot who drifts through life unaffected. It is about learning how to engage fully in life *without gripping it so tightly that you strangle the joy out of it.* It is the difference between admiring a beautiful flower and trying to preserve it forever by locking it in a glass case—only to watch it wither away.

In daily life, practicing non-attachment means showing up, giving your best, loving deeply, and pursuing your passions *without losing yourself in the process.* It means caring without clinging, investing without obsessing, and holding space for people and experiences without making them the foundation of your happiness.

The real challenge comes when life throws its inevitable curveballs. Plans fall apart, people disappoint us, opportunities slip through our fingers. The question is—do you let these moments wreck your peace, or do you roll with them? If you find yourself spiraling into frustration, anxiety, or a *full-blown existential meltdown* every time things do not go your way, that is a sign of attachment. And attachment is just a fancy word for *fear*—fear of losing, fear of change, fear of the unknown.

The key to non-attachment is recognizing those fears, calling them out, and consciously loosening your grip. It is not about detaching from life but about detaching from the illusion that you *need* things to be a certain way to be happy.

Cultivating a Flow Mindset. Letting Life Happen Without Trying to Manhandle It

Flow is that magical state where life feels effortless, like everything is clicking into place. It is not about having *zero* challenges—it is about not wasting your energy fighting against the ones that arise. The more you resist, control, or micromanage, the more you turn life into an uphill battle. The more you surrender to the natural rhythm of things, the more doors seem to open effortlessly.

To live in flow, start by ditching the illusion that you can—or should—control everything. No matter how much you plan, strategize, or overthink, there will always be factors outside of your hands. Instead of exhausting yourself trying to force things to happen on your timeline, practice being open to how life is unfolding.

Here is how to shift into a flow mindset:

- **Stop forcing.** If something is not working, pushing harder will not magically make it right. Sometimes, the best move is stepping back and allowing a new solution to emerge.

- **Let go of rigid timelines.** Life does not operate on your personal deadline. Things happen *when they are meant to,* not necessarily when you think they should.
- **Embrace the pivots.** Sometimes, what feels like a setback is actually a redirection toward something better. Be flexible enough to see the opportunity in the unexpected.
- **Stay present.** Flow happens when you are fully engaged in *this* moment, not obsessing over the future or rehashing the past. Be where you are, fully.

Flow is not about passively waiting for life to happen to you. It is about taking action *while staying open* to how things unfold. It is about working *with* life instead of trying to dominate it.

The Art of Surrender. How to Stop Fighting Reality and Actually Enjoy Life

Surrender gets a bad rap because it is often mistaken for giving up. But *real* surrender is not about passivity—it is about releasing the exhausting need to control every damn thing.

Surrender is choosing *peace over resistance.* It is accepting where you are *right now* instead of constantly wishing things were different. It is letting go of the mental tug-of-war between "what is" and "what should be." It is *trusting the process*—even when you do not understand it.

Why is surrender so powerful?

- It stops you from wasting energy on things you cannot change.
- It shifts you from stress mode to problem-solving mode.
- It allows you to adapt instead of self-destructing when things go sideways.
- It creates space for better things to enter your life instead of clinging to what is not working.

Practicing surrender does not mean you stop having goals, dreams, or desires. It just means you hold them *lightly.* You do the work, put in the effort, and then release the death grip on how it *has* to play out. You trust that if something is meant for you, it will happen—and if it is not, something better is coming.

Trusting the Process. Because Fighting Reality is a Losing Game

Life is unpredictable. Sometimes it is a smooth ride; other times, it feels like a bad reality show where everything goes wrong at once. The trick is to stop expecting life to go *exactly* as planned and start trusting that even the detours have a purpose.

Trusting the process does not mean sitting around and hoping everything magically works out. It means having faith in your ability to *handle* whatever comes your way. It is knowing that every challenge, setback, or delay is part of your evolution—even if it does not make sense yet.

How do you trust the process?

- **Stop assuming you know best.** The universe has a way of orchestrating things beyond what you can see.
- **Look back at past "failures."** How many times did something not work out, only to lead you somewhere better? Exactly.
- **Remind yourself that nothing is permanent.** Whatever you are stressing over today will not matter in five years. Keep perspective.
- **Let go of needing answers right now.** Some things only make sense in hindsight. Accept the uncertainty instead of fighting it.

Final Thoughts. Living With Detachment and Flow Without Becoming a Walking Hallmark Card

Living with detachment and flow is not about sitting in a lotus position and humming your way through life. It is about learning how to engage with life without losing yourself in it. It is about giving your best without letting results define you. It is about trusting that you are exactly where you need to be—even when it does not feel like it.

So loosen your grip. Stop trying to control every outcome. Be present. Roll with the punches. Let life unfold.

Because the moment you stop *forcing*, you start *living*.

Exercises and Journal Prompts. Your Emotional Decluttering Toolkit

Letting go is one of those things that sounds great in theory but can feel overwhelming in practice—kind of like deciding to clean out your closet only to end up sitting on the floor surrounded by a mountain of old clothes, feeling personally victimized by your past fashion choices. But just like tidying up your physical space can make you feel lighter and more in control, decluttering your emotional world has the same effect.

Below are some exercises and journal prompts to help you identify what's weighing you down, along with guided meditations and breathwork techniques to help you let that shit go. Think of this as your emotional spring cleaning, minus the dust bunnies.

Exercises to Identify What Needs to Go

1. The Letting Go Inventory. What Stays and What Gets the Boot?

Grab a notebook and make three columns: "Relationships," "Beliefs," and "Habits." Under each category, list out anything that no longer feels aligned with the person you are becoming. Be brutally honest. Who drains your energy? What outdated beliefs keep you playing small? What habits are keeping you stuck?

Now, go through and highlight the top three things in each category that feel *especially* heavy. These are your priority evictions. You don't have to let them all go overnight, but acknowledging them is the first step to reclaiming your peace.

2. The Daily Energy Scan. What Sucked the Life Out of You Today?

Every evening, take a few minutes to reflect on your day. Ask yourself:

- What moments drained my energy today?
- Was I holding onto something unnecessary?
- What could I have let go of to feel lighter?

This quick check-in helps you recognize patterns before they pile up into full-blown emotional clutter. The more you practice letting go in the small moments, the easier it gets to release the bigger stuff.

3. Object Release Ritual. Because Sometimes You Need a Physical Gesture

Pick one item in your home that carries emotional baggage. Maybe it's an ex's hoodie, a journal full of old heartbreak, or a gift from someone who turned out to be a toxic tornado. Whatever it is, acknowledge its place in your story, thank it for the lesson (if applicable), and let it go. Trash it, donate it, burn it (safely)—whatever feels right. The act of physically releasing something is a powerful way to signal to your brain that *you're done carrying that weight.*

Journal Prompts for Reflection and Release

If writing is your thing (or even if it's not), journaling can be a powerful way to process emotions and rewire your mindset. Here are some prompts to help you dig deep and start clearing out what no longer serves you:

- **What beliefs do I hold about myself that are no longer true?** What would happen if I stopped believing them?
- **What's one relationship in my life that feels heavy?** Is it worth healing, or is it time to move on?
- **What past experiences am I still carrying?** How are they affecting my present?
- **How do I handle things when they don't go my way?** What would happen if I loosened my grip and allowed life to unfold?
- **What does surrender look like to me?** How can I practice surrender in a way that still feels empowering?

These aren't one-and-done questions. Revisit them as needed, especially when you feel stuck. Sometimes, the simple act of writing things out helps you realize how ready you actually are to move forward.

Guided Meditation and Breathwork to Assist in Letting Go

Sometimes, words aren't enough—you need to physically and energetically *release* what's weighing you down. These techniques can help you do just that:

1. Breath of Release. Exhaling the Bullshit

- Sit comfortably and take a deep breath in through your nose. Imagine you're inhaling calm, peace, and fresh energy.
- As you exhale through your mouth, visualize all your stress, fears, and negativity leaving your body.

- Repeat for a few minutes, each breath getting deeper, each exhale carrying away the weight you no longer need.

It sounds simple, but don't underestimate the power of your breath—it's like hitting a mental reset button.

2. Letting Go Visualization. Watch It Float Away

- Close your eyes and picture yourself standing on a hilltop with a breathtaking view.
- In your hand, you hold a balloon. Inside the balloon is whatever you need to release—an old hurt, a limiting belief, a situation that's out of your control.
- When you're ready, open your hand and watch the balloon float away, getting smaller and smaller until it disappears completely.
- Feel the lightness in your body as you let go.

This practice is a great way to *physically feel* the act of release without needing to change anything in your external world.

3. Body Scan for Release. Because Stress Loves to Squat in Your Muscles

- Lie down and close your eyes.
- Start at your toes and work your way up, focusing on each body part. Notice any tension.
- With each inhale, imagine sending fresh energy to those tense areas.
- With each exhale, visualize the tension melting away.

By the time you reach the top of your head, you should feel noticeably lighter—almost like you just got a full-body massage without the awkward small talk.

Moving Forward with Lightness. Because Life is Too Short to Carry Extra Baggage

If there's one thing I hope you take away from this chapter, it's that *letting go is not just a feel-good concept—it's a survival skill.* If you want to grow, evolve, and actually enjoy your life, you have to be willing to drop the dead weight.

Why Letting Go is the Ultimate Growth Hack

Releasing what no longer serves you is like clearing space on your phone—it makes room for new apps (or, in this case, *new experiences, opportunities, and relationships*). Holding on to outdated thoughts, resentments, or toxic connections only slows you down. The more you let go, the lighter you move through life.

Letting go is not something you do *once* and then check off your list—it's a lifelong practice. Life will keep tossing new attachments, expectations, and emotional baggage your way, and each time, you'll get another chance to practice the fine art of *not letting it own you.* Think of it as emotional yoga: the goal is to get flexible enough that when life throws you curveballs, you *bend* instead of *break.*

Embracing the Freedom of Letting Go

There's nothing quite like the moment you realize you've finally released something that was weighing you down. It's like stepping into fresh air after being stuck in a stuffy room for way too long.

Letting go doesn't mean you don't care—it means you care enough to prioritize *your* peace, *your* growth, and *your* happiness. It means you trust that whatever is meant for you will stay, and whatever isn't will naturally drift away.

So take a deep breath, shake off the weight of everything you no longer need, and step forward with lightness. This is your life, and you don't need to carry a damn thing that isn't yours anymore.

This is just the beginning of something lighter, freer, and so much better.

Chapter 11

The Journey Continues

"Living your truth is the most liberating act of self-love—it's where authenticity meets courage, and where your soul finally feels at home." —Jamie

Just when you think you've got life all figured out, it loves to throw in a curveball—because what's an adventure without a few unexpected plot twists? If you thought this journey was leading to some grand, perfectly wrapped-up conclusion where everything makes sense and all your problems vanish, think again. Life doesn't work like that. And honestly? That's what makes it so damn exciting.

This chapter isn't about tying everything up with a neat little bow and calling it a day. Nope, we're just getting started. Your soul's journey isn't some one-and-done experience—it's an ever-evolving, wild, sometimes messy, always meaningful adventure. Think of it as an endless road trip, full of unexpected detours, scenic surprises, and the occasional pothole that makes you question all your life choices (because, of course).

We've been through a lot together—unpacking authenticity, facing fears, finding peace, and learning how to let go. But here's the thing: *this ride never really ends.* Life will keep throwing opportunities, lessons, and the occasional sucker punch your way. And that's the magic of it. Every twist and turn is another chance to grow, connect more deeply, and move forward with curiosity, courage, and—when needed—a well-timed expletive.

In this chapter, we're diving into how to keep that momentum going. How to stay open, keep evolving, and embrace whatever comes next with grace, grit, and maybe even a little humor. This isn't the end of the journey—it's just the next chapter. And you, my friend, are fully equipped to handle whatever's coming, armed with all the wisdom, resilience, and wit you've gathered along the way. So, let's get into it.

Living Your Truth Daily: Making Your Growth Stick

So, you've journeyed through the messy, beautiful, gut-wrenching, and soul-expanding work of self-discovery. You've faced your shadows, shattered old beliefs, and maybe even shed some tears (or screamed into a pillow—we don't judge here). You've picked up some pretty powerful insights along the way. But now comes the real challenge—*bringing all that wisdom into your everyday life.*

It's one thing to have a mind-blowing epiphany while meditating, journaling, or staring dramatically out of a window on a rainy day. It's another thing entirely to apply those insights when real life happens— when someone tests your patience, when self-doubt creeps in, when fear of judgment tries to pull you back into old habits. This is where the real work begins.

Living your truth isn't about making some massive, life-altering change overnight (unless that's your thing—then by all means, go for it). It's about the small, everyday choices that align with the person you've fought so hard to become. It's about waking up and deciding, *Today, I choose to be true to myself*—even if that just means speaking your mind, wearing the weird earrings you love, setting a boundary without apologizing, or saying "no" to something that doesn't feel right.

Because let's be real—what's the point of all this self-discovery if you keep your truth locked up in a journal or only bring it out during deep, wine-fueled conversations? This is your permission slip to start **living** what you've learned, letting it breathe, and allowing it to shape the way you move through the world—one badass, intentional step at a time.

How to Actually Live Your Truth—Because Epiphanies Don't Mean Shit Without Action

1. Listen to Your Gut and Act on It

Your intuition isn't some fluffy, abstract concept—it's your built-in BS detector. You've spent a lot of time reconnecting with yourself, learning to trust your instincts, and figuring out what truly aligns with you. Now, it's time to actually *listen* to that inner voice and act on it.

That means saying no when something feels off, even if it's uncomfortable. It means following the pull toward what excites and energizes you, even if it doesn't make logical sense to anyone else. It means trusting that you *do* know what's best for you, and not waiting for external validation before making a move.

2. Stop Shrinking Yourself to Make Others Comfortable

If you've spent any part of your life dimming your light, playing small, or twisting yourself into a version of you that makes *other* people comfortable, it's time to cut that shit out.

You don't have to explain your choices to people who don't get it. You don't have to apologize for growing, evolving, or becoming the person you were always meant to be. If your truth makes someone else uncomfortable, that's their issue—not yours. Keep shining. Keep showing up as your full, unapologetic self. The right people will celebrate you, and the wrong ones will weed themselves out.

3. Make Decisions That Align With Your Values

Living your truth means making choices that actually reflect who you *are*—not who the world expects you to be. This is where you get to put all that inner work to the test.

Before making a decision, ask yourself:

- *Is this in alignment with what I truly want, or am I just doing it to please someone else?*
- *Does this choice honor my boundaries, my needs, and my well-being?*
- *Am I doing this out of fear, guilt, or obligation?*

If something doesn't align, don't do it. If it feels forced, let it go. Your values are your internal compass—trust them.

4. Own Your Story—Even the Messy Parts

Living authentically means embracing **all** of who you are. That includes the mistakes, the lessons, the weird quirks, and the moments you wish you could rewrite. Every single part of your journey has shaped you, and there is power in owning it.

You don't have to pretend to have it all together. You don't have to hide the struggles that made you stronger. The more real you are, the more you attract people and opportunities that align with your truth.

5. Keep Growing, Keep Evolving

You don't just "arrive" at authenticity and call it a day. Life is constantly shifting, and so are you. What's true for you today might change a year from now—and that's okay.

Stay curious. Keep learning. Keep challenging yourself. The more you evolve, the more your truth deepens. Stay open to new insights, new experiences, and new versions of yourself.

The Truth About Living Your Truth

Living authentically isn't always easy. There will be moments when it feels like a battle—when fear, doubt, or the opinions of others try to pull you back into old habits. But here's what I want you to remember:

- **Your truth is worth fighting for.**
- **You don't owe anyone a version of yourself that makes them comfortable.**
- **You have permission to change, grow, and evolve as many times as you need to.**
- **The people who truly love you will love the real you, not the watered-down version.**

So, step into who you are with confidence. Speak your truth. Take up space. Own your journey.

This is just the beginning. You're not here to live a half-assed, muted-down version of life. You're here to experience the full, unapologetic, *soul-aligned* adventure that is uniquely yours.

So go live it. **Loudly. Boldly. Authentically.**

Making It Stick: Bringing Your Growth into Everyday Life

Alright, you've done the work. You've unpacked the heavy baggage, let go of what no longer serves you, and maybe even had a few life-altering *aha* moments. But now comes the real test—how do you actually integrate all this into your daily routine without it feeling like another chore on your never-ending to-do list? The answer: *You weave it into the fabric of your everyday life, one small, intentional step at a time.*

The goal here isn't to turn your life into a rigid self-improvement checklist. It's about making these practices second nature so that you're not just *thinking* about your truth—you're *living* it. And the best part? It doesn't have to be complicated. In fact, it can be fun, freeing, and surprisingly effortless once you get into the rhythm of it.

Practical Ways to Live What You've Learned

1. Start Small with Morning Intentions

The way you start your day sets the tone for everything that follows. Before you even roll out of bed, take a moment to set an intention—something simple that aligns with your growth. It could be:

- *"I will speak my truth without fear today."*
- *"I will respond to challenges with curiosity instead of frustration."*
- *"I will show up as my most authentic self."*

Write it down, say it out loud, or just hold it in your mind as you sip your coffee. Think of it as your personal theme for the day, anchoring you in what matters most.

2. Turn the Mundane into Mindfulness

Mindfulness isn't just for meditation cushions and yoga classes. You can practice it while brushing your teeth, making coffee, or sitting in traffic. The trick is to *pay attention*.

- Instead of rushing through your morning routine, actually **notice** the sensations—how warm the water feels, how the coffee smells, how your body wakes up.
- During your commute, take a deep breath and check in with yourself: *How am I feeling? Am I carrying stress from yesterday?*
- While eating, actually **taste** your food instead of inhaling it while scrolling through your phone.

These small moments of presence create a ripple effect, keeping you grounded and connected throughout the day.

3. Keep a Gratitude Reality Check

Gratitude isn't about toxic positivity or pretending everything is perfect. It's about *noticing* the good, even when life feels messy. Every evening, write down (or say out loud) three things you're grateful for.

- *"I had a great conversation with an old friend."*
- *"I honored my boundaries today."*
- *"I laughed really hard at something stupid, and it felt good."*

The more you focus on what's working, the more room you create for even better things to flow into your life.

4. Boundaries: Your Daily Act of Self-Respect

If you take *one* thing from this journey, let it be this: **Boundaries are not rude, selfish, or optional.** They are necessary. Period.

- Don't respond to texts immediately just because someone expects you to.
- Decline invitations that drain you instead of energizing you.
- Walk away from conversations that feel like emotional quicksand.

Every time you enforce a boundary, you're reinforcing the message that *your energy, time, and peace matter.*

5. Check In with Yourself Like You Would a Friend

You check on your friends, your pets, and even your houseplants. Why not check in on *yourself?* Take a few minutes at lunch or before bed to reflect:

- *"Did I stay true to myself today?"*

- *"Where did I compromise my truth, and why?"*
- *"What do I need more of? Less of?"*

These quick check-ins help you course-correct before things get too off track.

6. Play, Laugh, and Let Yourself Be a Little Ridiculous

Newsflash: *Growth isn't supposed to be serious all the time.* If you're not making space for joy, then what's the point?

- Dance in your kitchen.
- Sing obnoxiously in the car.
- Try something new with zero expectations of being good at it.

Play is a direct line to authenticity. The more you let yourself *be*, the more naturally you'll embody your truth.

7. Give Yourself a Freaking Break

There will be days when you totally nail it—when you feel aligned, at peace, and completely in flow. And then there will be days when you snap at someone, ignore your intuition, or fall into old patterns. *That's normal.* The key is to **not** spiral into self-criticism.

When you slip up, acknowledge it, learn from it, and move the hell on. This is a *journey*, not a race.

How to Stay True to Yourself When the World Has Other Plans

Living your truth sounds great—until external pressures come crashing in like a rogue wave, trying to pull you back into old patterns. Maybe it's societal expectations, family opinions, or just the general fear of judgment. Either way, it's easy to feel like you're swimming against the tide.

So, how do you stay the course when the world is pushing you in a different direction?

1. Get Crystal Clear on Your Core Values

Your values are your *inner compass*. When life gets chaotic, they guide you back home. If you don't know what yours are, take some time to reflect:

- What qualities are most important to you? (Honesty? Freedom? Creativity? Stability?)
- What makes you feel *alive* versus what drains you?
- What do you *not* want to compromise on?

Once you know your values, decisions become easier—because you'll instantly recognize when something *doesn't* align.

2. Master the Art of Saying No

Saying no isn't just a skill—it's a damn *superpower*. The sooner you get comfortable using it, the freer you'll feel. You don't owe anyone an explanation, a justification, or a dissertation on *why* you're declining something. A simple, "That doesn't work for me" is enough.

3. Surround Yourself with People Who Get It

You are *not* required to keep people in your life just because they've always been there. If someone constantly dismisses your growth, disrespects your boundaries, or makes you feel like you have to shrink yourself, it's time to reevaluate their place in your life.

Find your people. The ones who *celebrate* your truth, who make space for your evolution, and who love the real you—not just the version that's convenient for them.

4. Trust Yourself More Than the Noise

The world will always have opinions. Society will always have expectations. But at the end of the day, *you* are the only one who has to live with your choices.

When in doubt, tune out the noise and tune into yourself.

- If something doesn't feel right, it probably isn't.
- If you have to convince yourself to stay, it's probably time to go.
- If you're trying to be someone you're not, you'll never be truly happy.

Your gut *knows*. Trust it.

Final Thoughts: Owning Your Truth Like the Badass You Are

Living your truth isn't about being perfect. It's about being **real**— messy, evolving, beautifully imperfect, *real*. It's about making choices that align with *you*, even when it's hard. It's about honoring your needs, trusting your intuition, and giving yourself permission to live fully, unapologetically, and authentically.

So keep going. Keep growing. Keep choosing yourself.

And if anyone has a problem with that?

That's a *them* problem, not a *you* problem.

How to Make Authenticity, Mindfulness, and Gratitude a Natural Part of Your Everyday Life

Incorporating authenticity, mindfulness, and gratitude into your daily routine doesn't have to feel like an extreme lifestyle makeover. No one is expecting you to shave your head, move to a mountaintop, and dedicate your life to silent meditation (unless that's your thing—then, by all means, rock on). The truth is, making these things second nature is way easier than you think—it just takes a little intention and some consistency.

The secret? **Stop overcomplicating it.** You don't need a three-hour morning ritual, a color-coded gratitude journal, or the perfect yoga playlist to live in alignment. You just need to build small habits that bring these practices into your daily life without turning them into another obligation.

1. Start Small with Intentional Choices

Living authentically isn't about some big dramatic *Eat, Pray, Love* moment where you throw your life into chaos just to "find yourself." It's about making small, consistent choices that align with your true self.

- Wear the clothes that make you feel like *you* (yes, even if that means rocking those ridiculous but beloved fuzzy socks in public).
- Speak your truth, even in tiny ways, like saying "actually, I don't like sushi" instead of pretending to enjoy it to fit in.
- Choose activities, people, and conversations that energize you instead of drain you.

The little choices add up. And before you know it, *bam*—you're living an authentic life without even trying.

2. Mindfulness in the Everyday, Not Just on a Yoga Mat

You don't need an hour of meditation to practice mindfulness. Some of the best moments of awareness happen in the most mundane parts of your day. Try this instead:

- When drinking your morning coffee, actually *taste* it instead of chugging it while doom-scrolling.

- When you're driving, stop mentally writing your grocery list and just *drive*. Notice the scenery, feel your hands on the wheel, turn up the music, and *be present*.
- During conversations, *listen* instead of mentally preparing your response.

The goal is to stop living on autopilot. You don't need a retreat—you just need to show up for the moment you're in.

3. Gratitude, but Make It Easy

Gratitude doesn't require a full production. No one is judging you for not keeping a perfectly curated "gratitude journal." Just make it a habit to *notice the good*.

- The sun felt amazing on your face? *Noted.*
- Someone made you laugh so hard you snorted? *A moment to appreciate.*
- You got through an entire day without wanting to throw your phone into a lake? *A true victory.*

If you want to write things down, great. If not, just *acknowledge* them as they happen. Gratitude is a perspective shift, not a homework assignment.

4. Make It a Habit Without Overthinking It

Let's be honest—if something feels like *work*, you're going to resist doing it. So instead of making mindfulness, authenticity, and gratitude another thing on your checklist, **sneak it into your life naturally**:

- Stack habits: Set an intention while brushing your teeth. Do a one-minute breathing exercise while waiting for your coffee. List three things you're grateful for before bed.

- Attach meaning to small actions: Saying "no" when something doesn't feel right? That's an act of authenticity. Taking a deep breath before reacting? That's mindfulness in action.
- Keep it light: Living with purpose doesn't mean being serious all the time. Laugh, dance in your kitchen, and embrace the ridiculousness of life.

The goal isn't perfection. It's progress. And trust me, when you make it *easy*, you're way more likely to stick with it.

The Never-Ending Glow-Up: Continuous Growth and the Journey of the Soul

So you've put in the work, done the inner reflection, and maybe even shocked yourself with some *holy shit*, I've really changed moments. But here's the thing about growth—it *never stops*. Just when you think you've got it all figured out, life smirks and says, "Oh, you're comfortable? Cute. Here's a new challenge."

Personal and spiritual growth isn't a destination—it's an *endless expansion*. The moment you stop learning, evolving, and challenging yourself is the moment you start *stagnating*—and stagnation is the quickest way to turn your life into a monotonous loop of *blah*.

1. Growth Has No Finish Line—Get Used to It

There's no point where you suddenly "arrive" and life is perfect. You will always be a work in progress, and that's actually a *good* thing.

- The lessons you learn at 30 will evolve when you hit 40.
- The beliefs you hold today might shift after new experiences.
- Who you are now isn't who you'll be five years from now—and that's *exciting*.

Instead of aiming for some elusive version of "completion," embrace the *ongoing transformation*. It's what keeps life interesting.

2. Stay Open to Change, Even When It's Uncomfortable

Here's a hard truth: Growth often feels like absolute chaos before it feels like progress.

- Change rarely happens in a neat, tidy, step-by-step way.
- Sometimes it feels like you're completely lost before you find clarity.
- The things you once clung to will become things you outgrow—and that's okay.

The key is **not resisting it**. The more you fight change, the harder you make it for yourself. Trust that every shift, every detour, and every unexpected challenge is shaping you into the person you're meant to become.

3. Cultivate Curiosity—It's the Key to Everything

Want to stay in a constant state of growth without feeling exhausted by it? **Stay curious.**

- Ask more questions.
- Try new things just for the hell of it.
- Read books on topics you know nothing about.
- Surround yourself with people who challenge your perspective.

Curiosity keeps your mind sharp, your soul engaged, and your life *interesting*. The second you think you have it all figured out, remind yourself: *there's always more to learn.*

Navigating Life's Never-Ending Plot Twists

Life is basically one long, unpredictable novel with twists you *definitely* didn't see coming. But guess what? **You're the main character, and you get to decide how the story plays out.**

- Challenges will keep coming, but now you know how to handle them.
- Change will keep knocking on your door, but now you're ready to embrace it.
- Life will keep throwing unexpected opportunities your way, and now you have the *courage* to say "yes" when it feels right.

This journey isn't about having all the answers. It's about staying open, evolving, and rolling with whatever comes your way.

So take a deep breath, trust the process, and *keep going*.

Because the best part of this whole adventure?

The story is still being written.

How to View New Challenges as Opportunities for Further Growth and Self-Discovery

Life has a way of throwing curveballs when you least expect them—because apparently, it enjoys keeping things interesting. But here's the deal: challenges aren't just annoying roadblocks designed to ruin your plans. They're actually stepping stones to a stronger, wiser, and more badass version of yourself.

Instead of defaulting to frustration or resistance, try flipping the script. Ask yourself, *What is this trying to teach me? How is this challenge stretching me in ways I wouldn't have chosen on my own?* This shift in mindset transforms obstacles from soul-sucking energy drains into some of your greatest teachers.

Growth isn't found in the smooth, easy moments—it's built in the trenches. The discomfort? That's where the real magic happens. Every challenge is a new chapter in your journey, shaping you in ways you never expected. So next time life pulls a fast one, take a deep breath, roll up your sleeves, and remind yourself: *This is just another opportunity to level up.*

Practical Strategies for Staying Resilient and Adaptable

Resilience and adaptability aren't just nice traits to have—they're survival skills in this wild, unpredictable world. Life is going to keep throwing unexpected twists your way, and your ability to roll with the punches will determine how much joy, peace, and success you experience.

1. Cultivate a Flexible Mindset

- **Make Change Your Friend:** Fighting change is like arguing with gravity—pointless and exhausting. The sooner you accept that change is inevitable, the more energy you'll have to actually *work* with it instead of against it.
- **Reframe the Struggle:** Instead of seeing setbacks as failures, see them as valuable lessons. Ask yourself, *What is this teaching me? How can I use this experience to grow?* A growth mindset turns obstacles into stepping stones instead of roadblocks.

2. Build a Strong Support System

- **Surround Yourself with Real Ones:** Keep close the people who uplift, encourage, and challenge you in the best way possible. Your energy is precious—stop wasting it on people who drain you.
- **Don't Be Afraid to Ask for Help:** Resilience doesn't mean doing it all alone. Leaning on the right people—whether it's friends, mentors, or a therapist—can give you the clarity and strength you need to move forward.

3. Stay Mindful and Emotionally Aware

- **Pause Before Reacting:** When things get stressful, take a breath before responding. A single mindful moment can keep you from spiraling into unnecessary drama or frustration.
- **Acknowledge, Don't Suppress:** Resilience isn't about bottling things up. Honor your emotions, process them, and then decide how to move forward without letting them control you.

4. Take Care of Your Body, Not Just Your Mind

- **Move Your Body:** Physical activity isn't just about looking good—it's one of the best ways to clear mental fog, release stress, and boost your mood.
- **Prioritize Sleep and Fuel Wisely:** Your body is your vehicle for navigating life's challenges—don't run it on fumes and junk fuel. Treat yourself like the high-performance machine you are.

5. Break It Down and Celebrate Small Wins

- **One Step at a Time:** Big challenges feel overwhelming when you look at them as a whole. Break them down into small, manageable steps, and tackle them one by one.
- **Celebrate Every Victory:** Even tiny wins matter. Acknowledging your progress keeps you motivated and reminds you that, yes, you *are* handling this.

6. Keep a Growth Mindset

- **Everything is a Lesson:** Whether it's a win or a loss, every experience is a chance to learn something new about yourself. The goal isn't perfection—it's progress.
- **Stay Curious:** Try new things, explore different perspectives, and always be open to growth. Curiosity keeps life interesting and keeps you moving forward.

The key to resilience? It's not about avoiding the waves—it's about learning how to surf.

Staying Connected to Your Inner Self

In the chaos of everyday life, it's easy to lose sight of your inner voice—the one that actually knows what's best for you. Between societal expectations, endless distractions, and everyone's unsolicited opinions, staying in tune with yourself takes some real effort. But when you make it a priority, life feels less like a constant hustle for approval and more like a path that actually *fits* you.

1. Make Self-Check-Ins a Daily Habit

- **Quick Daily Reflections:** Pause throughout the day to ask yourself: *How am I feeling? Am I acting in alignment with my truth?* These mini check-ins help keep you grounded.
- **Weekly Deep Dives:** Set aside time each week to reflect on what's working, what's not, and where you need to make adjustments.
- **Monthly Alignment Reviews:** Take a bigger-picture look at your life each month. Are you moving in the direction you want? If not, what needs to shift?

2. Use Mindfulness, Meditation, and Journaling to Stay Grounded

- **Mindfulness in the Everyday:** Presence isn't reserved for meditation cushions—practice it while you're eating, walking, or even washing the dishes. The more aware you are of *now*, the less time you spend spiraling about things outside your control.
- **Meditation for Clarity:** Even five minutes a day of quiet reflection can work wonders for tuning out the noise and reconnecting with yourself.

- **Journaling to Process and Reflect:** Writing things down helps bring clarity. Your journal is a judgment-free zone where you can be completely honest with yourself.

3. Strengthen Your Intuition and Actually Listen to It

- **Turn Down the Noise:** Create moments of stillness so your intuition can actually be heard. It's always speaking—you just have to be quiet enough to listen.
- **Trust Your First Instincts:** Your gut often knows the truth before your logical mind catches up. Learn to trust those initial feelings.
- **Be Patient with the Process:** Sometimes the answers don't come right away. Trust that the clarity you need will arrive when it's meant to.

Final Thoughts: You've Got This

Let's be real—life isn't going to suddenly stop throwing challenges your way just because you've done some inner work. But the difference now? **You know how to handle them.**

- You understand that challenges aren't here to break you— they're here to shape you.
- You have the tools to stay resilient, adaptable, and grounded no matter what comes your way.
- You trust yourself enough to navigate the unknown with confidence.

And perhaps most importantly? **You've realized that growth never really ends.**

The journey of becoming your most authentic, empowered self isn't a straight line. It's a wild, winding road with highs, lows, and everything in between. But through it all, you are learning, evolving, and becoming exactly who you're meant to be.

So take a deep breath, step forward, and embrace the adventure. Because this? This is just the beginning.

Evolving Your Purpose Over Time

Life isn't static, and neither is your soul's purpose. What lights you up at one stage of life might feel like an ill-fitting pair of jeans at another. (And let's be honest, if you're still rocking your favorite outfit from high school, I salute you.) Growth isn't about staying the same—it's about evolving, refining, and stepping into new callings as you expand into your fullest self.

1. Recognizing That Your Soul's Purpose Evolves With You

Your purpose isn't some carved-in-stone life mission you have to uncover like a buried treasure—it's more like a compass, guiding you through shifting landscapes. As you gain wisdom, face new challenges, and experience life's highs and lows, your purpose naturally shifts too.

Maybe in your twenties, you were all about climbing the career ladder, but now? Maybe you crave more creativity, more freedom, more depth. Or perhaps you once defined yourself by one passion, but now you feel pulled in an entirely new direction. Guess what? That's *normal*. Your purpose is meant to expand as you do.

So, instead of clinging to an outdated version of yourself, let your purpose evolve the way it's meant to. Trust that every chapter of your journey has its place—even the messy ones.

2. How to Embrace These Shifts Without Freaking Out

Change is a lot like jumping into cold water—your first instinct might be to tense up and resist, but if you lean into it, you'll realize it's actually refreshing as hell. Here's how to embrace the evolution of your purpose with more curiosity and less fear:

- **Stay Open-Minded:** Instead of clinging to what was, ask yourself, *What new possibilities are calling me?* A beginner's mindset will help you navigate change with excitement instead of dread.
- **Make Space for the New:** Just like cleaning out your closet, sometimes you have to let go of the old to make room for the new. Releasing outdated goals or identities isn't a loss—it's an upgrade.
- **Find Your Anchors:** When change feels overwhelming, ground yourself in what remains constant—your values, your core strengths, and the things that bring you joy. Purpose may evolve, but who you *are* at your core stays steady.
- **Seek Support:** Talk to mentors, coaches, or those who've been through similar transitions. A fresh perspective can help you see the bigger picture when you're too deep in the weeds.

When you allow your purpose to shift naturally, you stop forcing yourself to fit into a box that no longer serves you—and that's where real freedom begins.

3. Real-Life Stories of Purpose Evolving Over Time

Throughout history, people have pivoted their lives in ways that changed not only their own paths but also the world.

- **Julia Child** didn't discover her passion for cooking until her late thirties—after a career in government intelligence. And let's be real, where would the world be without her buttery brilliance?
- **Vera Wang** didn't design her first wedding dress until she was 40. Now, she's *the* name in bridal fashion.
- **Oprah** started as a news anchor before shifting into a role that aligned with her true gift—helping people find meaning and transformation.

The point? You don't have to have it all figured out from the start. In fact, the best stories are the ones that take unexpected turns.

4. My Own Evolution: From Sales to Spiritual Healing and Everything in Between

For years, I was all about connection—understanding people, anticipating their needs, and delivering results. Sales and customer service came naturally to me. I was damn good at it. But the deeper I went into my career, the more I realized that success on paper wasn't the same as fulfillment in my soul. Something felt *off*.

That feeling—the nagging sense that I was meant for something more—only got louder. And if there's one thing I've learned, it's that when your soul keeps whispering (or screaming) at you for change, you better listen.

I had always been drawn to aesthetics and beauty, but making the leap from corporate life to advanced aesthetics felt terrifying. Still, I couldn't ignore the pull. So I trained, learned, and embraced the artistry of skincare and cosmetics. At the same time, my personal journey took me deeper into spirituality, healing, and personal transformation. The more I healed my own wounds, the more I realized I wanted to help others do the same.

That's when *Skull Sugar Cosmetics* was born—not just a beauty brand, but a reflection of self-expression, empowerment, and embracing both the light and the dark within ourselves. My purpose had shifted *again*, expanding beyond external beauty to deeper healing—helping others reconnect with themselves on a soul level.

Looking back, every step of my journey made sense—even the ones that didn't at the time. Each career shift, each personal challenge, each unexpected pivot was leading me here. And I know this isn't my final destination—because purpose is *always* evolving.

5. How You Can Adapt Your Purpose as You Grow

So, how do *you* navigate your own shifting sense of purpose without losing your mind? Start here:

- **Check In With Yourself Regularly:** What lights you up *now*? What drains you? If something that once excited you now feels like a chore, it might be time for a change.
- **Give Yourself Permission to Change:** You are *not* obligated to be the same person you were five years ago, last year, or even last month. Growth is a sign you're doing something right.
- **Follow What Feels Aligned:** Pay attention to what energizes you. Passion doesn't always come with a neon sign—sometimes, it's a quiet pull in a new direction. Follow it.
- **Experiment Without Pressure:** You don't have to make huge life-altering decisions overnight. Explore new interests, take small steps, and see what clicks.

6. The Beauty of an Evolving Purpose

The idea that you have *one* singular purpose for your entire life? Outdated. Purpose is fluid. It changes as you change, grows as you grow, and shifts as you uncover new layers of yourself.

One chapter of your life may be about building a career, another about personal healing, another about teaching or giving back. Some seasons are about expansion, others about rest and reflection. And every single one of them is *valid*.

Your job isn't to cling to an old version of yourself out of fear—it's to trust that as you evolve, your purpose will too.

So, if you're feeling that nudge for something more, listen to it. You don't have to have all the answers yet—just the courage to take the next step.

Because your journey? It's still unfolding. And the best part? *You get to decide where it leads next.*

Next Steps: Continuing the Journey

If you've made it this far, congratulations—you've done some serious inner work, and that's no small feat. But before you start thinking this is the end of your journey, let's be real—this is just the warm-up. The insights, tools, and practices you've picked up along the way? They're not just for this chapter of your life. They're the foundation for everything that comes next.

This isn't about checking off some cosmic to-do list and calling it a day. Personal growth isn't a destination—it's a never-ending road trip, complete with unexpected detours, surprise pit stops, and the occasional "What the hell am I doing?" moment. The key is to keep integrating what you've learned into your daily life—making sure your actions, choices, and mindset align with the person you're becoming.

But here's the best part: You don't have to do it perfectly. Growth isn't linear. Some days, you'll feel completely in sync with the universe, and other days, you'll be stress-eating snacks in your pajamas wondering what happened to your enlightened self. And that's okay. Keep going, keep learning, and keep laughing at the absurdity of it all.

How to Keep Growing Without Losing Your Mind

- **Stay Open to New Opportunities** – Life isn't done teaching you yet. Keep saying yes to new experiences, even if they're out of your comfort zone. Sometimes, the best lessons come from the least expected places.
- **Make Reflection a Habit** – Keep checking in with yourself. What's working? What's not? Adjust accordingly. Growth is an ongoing process, not a one-time epiphany.
- **Surround Yourself with the Right People** – Find the ones who inspire, challenge, and support you. Cut ties with anyone who keeps you stuck in old patterns. Your energy is precious— spend it wisely.
- **Keep a Sense of Humor** – Seriously. If you can't laugh at the chaos of life, it's going to be a long ride. Embrace the ridiculousness, and don't take yourself too seriously.

At the end of the day, your journey isn't about getting everything right. It's about staying curious, being brave enough to evolve, and allowing yourself the freedom to explore whatever comes next.

Further Reading, Practices, and Exploration to Keep You Inspired

If you're hungry for more (and let's be honest, growth is addictive), here are some books, practices, and experiences to deepen your understanding and keep you moving forward.

Books to Fuel Your Expansion

- **"The Power of Now" – Eckhart Tolle** – If you tend to overthink, this book will remind you that the only moment that matters is right now.

- **"The Untethered Soul" – Michael A. Singer** – Teaches you how to release the thoughts and emotions that keep you stuck. Deep but incredibly freeing.
- **"Big Magic" – Elizabeth Gilbert** – A love letter to creativity and embracing fear in a way that actually works for you.
- **"Daring Greatly" – Brené Brown** – For anyone who needs a pep talk on courage, vulnerability, and showing up fully in life.
- **"The Four Agreements" – Don Miguel Ruiz** – Simple, yet powerful, principles for living with more clarity, love, and integrity.

Practices to Keep You Centered

- **Daily Meditation** – Whether it's five minutes or thirty, meditation helps keep your mind from running wild. Apps like Insight Timer and Headspace are great for guidance.
- **Gratitude Journaling** – Each night, jot down three things you're grateful for. It's a small habit with big mindset benefits.
- **Mindful Movement** – Yoga, tai chi, or even just a slow, intentional walk. Moving with awareness helps keep you grounded.
- **Breathwork** – Deep breathing techniques can help release emotional tension and bring clarity when you feel stuck.
- **Creative Expression** – Write, paint, dance—whatever lights you up. Creativity isn't just an outlet, it's a gateway to deeper self-discovery.

Exploration: Expanding Your Worldview

- **Attend a Retreat or Workshop** – A weekend away focusing on spiritual growth, creativity, or self-care can be life-changing.

- **Immerse Yourself in New Cultures** – Travel, even if it's just to a different part of town. Seeing the world from a new perspective shifts everything.
- **Join a Like-Minded Community** – Whether it's a meditation group, a book club, or an online forum, being around people on a similar path keeps you inspired.
- **Volunteer for a Cause You Care About** – Giving your time and energy not only helps others but deepens your connection to your own sense of purpose.
- **Try New Spiritual Practices** – Tarot, sound healing, energy work—there's a whole world of spiritual tools out there. Explore what resonates with you.

Seeking Out New Experiences That Align With Your Evolving Purpose

Your purpose is never a one-and-done deal. It shifts, grows, and refines itself as you do. So how do you keep finding experiences that align with the person you're becoming?

1. Follow Your Curiosity

Your interests and passions are leading you somewhere—pay attention. That random thing you keep Googling? Maybe it's worth exploring.

2. Get Comfortable with Discomfort

Growth doesn't happen in the comfort zone. Be willing to try new things, even when they're intimidating. That's where the magic is.

3. Surround Yourself with Expanders

Spend time with people who challenge you, inspire you, and push you to think bigger. Their energy will rub off on you.

4. Commit to Lifelong Learning

Read, take classes, attend events—never stop expanding your mind. The more you learn, the more you discover about yourself.

5. Trust Your Intuition

Sometimes the best opportunities don't make logical sense. If something feels right, go with it.

6. Check In With Yourself Regularly

What excites you? What drains you? Adjust accordingly. Your purpose is a moving target—stay flexible.

7. Say Yes More Often

Even if it scares you. Especially if it scares you. Some of the best experiences come from taking chances you never planned on.

Celebrating the Journey So Far

Alright, let's take a second to appreciate how far you've come. Seriously—pause, take a breath, and give yourself a well-deserved pat on the back (or, if you prefer, a full-blown happy dance). Whether you've been sprinting, crawling, or somewhere in between, you've still made progress, and that's worth celebrating.

Reflecting on your journey isn't just about giving yourself credit (though, let's be real, you deserve it). It's about acknowledging the work you've put in—the baby steps, the bold leaps, the messy middles, and even the faceplants. Each moment of growth counts. Whether you've finally mastered the art of setting boundaries, learned to quiet your inner critic, or simply started being a little kinder to yourself, it all matters.

So how do you mark the milestones? Maybe it's treating yourself to a solo getaway, journaling about your progress, or just taking a moment to sit in gratitude for how much you've evolved. Whatever you do, make sure it's something that reminds you why you started this journey in the first place.

Celebrating isn't just about feeling good—it's about fueling yourself for what's ahead. The journey isn't over. In fact, it's only getting started. So, soak in the moment, and then get ready for all the exciting, unpredictable, and possibly life-changing adventures still to come.

Conclusion: The Journey Never Ends

If you thought this was the end of the road—think again. Personal growth isn't a final destination, a neat little bow you tie around your soul's evolution and call it a day. Nope, this is more like a never-ending TV series—just when you think you've wrapped up one season, the next one drops with new challenges, unexpected plot twists, and characters who may or may not test your patience.

But that's the beauty of it. Every new phase brings fresh lessons, new opportunities, and deeper levels of self-discovery. The trick is to stay open—to keep showing up, keep learning, and keep embracing the messy, wonderful, unpredictable adventure of life.

Sure, there will be moments when things don't go as planned. You might question everything, hit roadblocks, or find yourself on a detour you didn't see coming. But guess what? You've already proven you can handle it. You've got the tools, the awareness, and the resilience to navigate whatever comes next. And if all else fails, just take a deep breath, tap into that inner wisdom, and remind yourself that you're exactly where you need to be.

Reflection on the Journey: Key Takeaways

Before you go, let's take a moment to reflect on everything we've explored together.

- **Your journey is uniquely yours.** There's no "one right way" to grow, evolve, or heal. Your process is valid, no matter how fast or slow it unfolds.
- **Authenticity is everything.** When you align with your truth, life flows in ways you never imagined. Stay true to yourself, even when it's uncomfortable.
- **Letting go is a superpower.** Releasing what no longer serves you creates space for the things that do. It's not about loss—it's about freedom.
- **Challenges are just disguised growth opportunities.** When life throws you curveballs, ask, "What is this teaching me?" instead of "Why is this happening to me?"
- **You are always evolving.** Your purpose, passions, and desires will shift over time. Stay open to the process and trust where it leads you.

At the heart of it all, this journey isn't about reaching a perfect state of enlightenment. It's about embracing life fully—messy emotions, unexpected detours, and all. It's about showing up for yourself, trusting the unfolding, and finding joy in the ride.

So as you move forward, don't just focus on the destination. Celebrate the adventure. Let your soul guide you. Stay curious, stay open, and remember that you are always, always becoming.

A Heartfelt Thank You

Before you close this book, I just want to take a moment to say—**thank you.**

Thank you for showing up, for diving into this journey with an open heart, and for allowing me to walk alongside you through these pages. Writing this wasn't just about sharing insights and lessons—it was about creating a space where we could connect on a deeper level, where I could share my truth in the hopes that it would resonate with yours.

Your journey is uniquely yours, and I'm honored that you let me be a small part of it. My hope is that these words stay with you, that they remind you of your strength, your worth, and your ability to create a life that feels aligned and fulfilling. As you move forward, I hope you continue to grow, explore, and evolve in ways that light you up. May you always trust yourself, follow your soul's calling, and never stop seeking what makes you come alive. And remember—this is just the beginning. The best is always yet to come.

But before we part ways, I need to express my gratitude to the people who have shaped my own journey—those who have lifted me up, challenged me, and held space for me in ways I can never fully repay.

To my sister, Misti

We are the closest of siblings. You have been my rock through every heartbreak, every moment of doubt, and every relationship catastrophe I've thrown at you. Even when you were walking through your own grief, after losing your husband, you still had the strength to be there for me. You've never made me feel like my pain was too small to matter, even when yours was immeasurable. Thank you for your unwavering love, your wisdom, and your ability to talk me off the ledge—over and over again. I am endlessly grateful for you.

You've shown me what resilience looks like, what unconditional support feels like, and what it means to show up even when your own heart is breaking. You carry so much strength and grace, and yet you always make space for my mess, my chaos, and my healing. I don't know how I would have made it through some of life's darkest chapters without you by my side. You are not just my sister—you are my soul's constant, my forever safe place, and one of the greatest gifts I've ever been given. I love you to the moon and beyond!

To my dad

You were always there with a listening ear when I needed you most, never judging me during my battles with addiction—just loving me through it. Your compassion, your wisdom, and your steady presence meant everything when I felt lost. I hope you know how much that has shaped me and how grateful I am for you.

To my mom

Our relationship has had its ups and downs, but one thing has always remained true—I am deeply grateful to you for giving me life. That gift is something I will never take for granted. No matter where our paths have led, I recognize the part you played in my journey and how it helped shape who I've become. I love you. And with an open heart, I want you to know that I forgive you. I truly believe you did the best you could with what you had, and I honor the intention behind the choices you made, even when they were hard for me to understand.

To Dawn

For showing me what unconditional love looks like and for bringing so many wonderful souls into my life. Your presence has been a gift, and the love and kindness you have shared with me have left a lasting impact on my heart.

You've shown up in ways I didn't even know I needed, offering support, laughter, and a sense of belonging that has carried me through some of life's most difficult moments. You've taught me that family isn't always about blood—it's about who shows up with open arms and an open heart. I am a better, stronger, more whole version of myself because you were part of my story.

To those who challenged me

To the ones who tested my strength, who pushed me to my breaking points, and who forced me to grow even when I didn't want to—thank you. You showed me where I still had wounds to heal, where I was abandoning myself, and where I was confusing chaos for connection. You mirrored the parts of me that were still searching for validation, still trying to prove I was enough. Your actions, as painful as they were, cracked me open and led me straight to the parts of myself I had neglected for far too long.

To the men who broke my heart, thank you for teaching me the lessons I needed to learn. You revealed the difference between intensity and intimacy, between being chosen and truly cherished. Each goodbye carved out space for something greater—something rooted in respect, trust, and authenticity. Without you, I wouldn't have discovered my own worth, and I wouldn't have learned what real, healthy love looks like.

You were painful but necessary teachers, and I've finally graduated from your class.

To Justin

Your love is a safe place for me to land, even when my fears try to convince me otherwise. Your patience, your understanding, and the way you show up for me—especially when I'm tangled in my own doubts— mean more than I can ever put into words. Thank you for seeing me, for loving me, and for standing beside me as I navigate this wild journey.

You don't try to fix me or rush my healing—you simply hold space. You remind me that I am worthy, even when I question it myself. With you, I can exhale. I can soften. I can be all that I am without fear of being too much or not enough. That kind of love is rare, and I don't take it for granted. Thank you for being my anchor, my mirror, and my quiet strength when I forget my own.

To my soul siblings, Nyko and Mossy

You see me in ways that few people do. You challenge me, push me, hold up a mirror when I need it, and remind me that growth is a lifelong process. **Mossy**, your fierce heart and unwavering support have been a gift beyond measure. Your love, your truth, and the way you constantly challenge me to be better have helped shape the person I am today. **Nyko**, you have been there through so much, always lifting me up, always reminding me of my strength. We are constantly evolving, constantly healing, and constantly bringing out the best in one another—and I wouldn't have it any other way.

To my soul tribe

The ones who have held space for me, who have walked beside me, and who have encouraged my growth—you know who you are. Your presence in my life has been a gift, and I am forever grateful for the love and wisdom you've shared with me.

And finally, to **you**, the reader.

For being here, for showing up for yourself, for choosing growth, healing, and self-discovery. Thank you for allowing my words to be part of your journey. May you continue to seek, to grow, and to step fully into the truth of who you are.

With love and gratitude,
Jamie

Additional Resources

As you continue your journey of self-discovery and growth, here are some additional resources to support and inspire you. Whether you're looking to deepen your spiritual practice, explore new ideas, or keep the momentum going, these books, websites, and tools are great companions along the way.

Books for Personal and Spiritual Growth

Journey of My Soul: A Guided Journal – Jamie O'Neill
A powerful tool for self-reflection, designed to help you connect with your soul's purpose and navigate your healing journey.

Unbreakable: A Journey of Healing, Growth, and Self-Discovery – Jamie O'Neill
A deeply personal and inspiring guide to overcoming life's challenges, finding resilience, and stepping into your true power.

The Power of Now – Eckhart Tolle
A must-read for mindfulness and presence, helping you break free from overthinking and live fully in the moment.

The Four Agreements – Don Miguel Ruiz
Simple but powerful wisdom to transform your mindset and relationships through four life-changing principles.

Radical Acceptance – Tara Brach
A compassionate guide to letting go of self-judgment and embracing yourself exactly as you are.

The Untethered Soul – Michael A. Singer
A deep dive into inner freedom and breaking free from the thoughts and emotions that hold you back.

Big Magic – Elizabeth Gilbert
A fun, insightful read on embracing creativity and living fearlessly.

Nonviolent Communication – Marshall B. Rosenberg
A transformative approach to communication that fosters empathy, understanding, and deeper connections.

Websites and Digital Resources

Mindful.org – A hub for mindfulness articles, guided meditations, and practical tools for living with more awareness.

Tiny Buddha – Wisdom, quotes, and personal stories focused on happiness, mindfulness, and self-growth.

Headspace – A meditation and mindfulness app with guided sessions for stress relief, focus, and better sleep.

Tools and Practices for Growth

Meditation Apps: Calm, Insight Timer, and Headspace offer guided meditations, mindfulness exercises, and sleep support.

Journaling Tools: Use The Five-Minute Journal for structured reflection, or free-write your thoughts and emotions daily.

Yoga and Movement: Explore free yoga classes on YouTube, like Yoga with Adriene, or take a local class to connect mind and body.

Breathwork Practices: Try controlled breathing techniques to reduce stress, increase energy, and gain clarity.

Creative Exploration: Engage in painting, writing, music, or any form of artistic expression to connect with your inner self.

Bonus Meditations

Morning Intention-Setting Meditation

Purpose: To start the day with clarity and focus, setting positive intentions aligned with your soul's purpose.

Instructions:

- Find a comfortable seat, close your eyes, and take a few deep breaths.
- Feel yourself grounded and supported by the earth beneath you.
- As you inhale, set an intention for the day ahead. Examples: "Today, I will approach challenges with curiosity" or "I will practice self-compassion."
- Visualize your day unfolding with ease, clarity, and purpose.
- Repeat silently or aloud: "Today, I live with intention. I am open to the opportunities and lessons this day will bring."
- Take a final deep breath and open your eyes, carrying this intention into your day.

Letting Go Meditation

Purpose: To release past hurts, limiting beliefs, or anything that no longer serves your highest good.

Instructions:

- Sit in a quiet space and take several slow, deep breaths.
- Scan your body for tension and consciously breathe into those areas, releasing any discomfort.
- Bring to mind something you need to let go of—a past experience, an old belief, or lingering resentment.

- Picture it as an object in your hands, heavy and weighing you down.
- Now imagine yourself gently releasing it, watching it drift away until it disappears.
- Fill the empty space with a golden light, symbolizing peace and freedom.
- Repeat: "I release what no longer serves me. I am open to new opportunities and growth."
- Take a final breath and slowly return to the present moment.

Gratitude Meditation

Purpose: To cultivate a deep sense of gratitude and abundance.

Instructions:

- Sit comfortably and close your eyes, taking slow, deep breaths.
- Bring your focus to your heart, imagining it radiating warmth and openness.
- Think of three things you're grateful for today. Visualize each one in detail.
- Let the feeling of gratitude expand throughout your entire body.
- Repeat: "I am grateful for all the blessings in my life. My heart is open to receive and give love."
- Take another deep breath and open your eyes, carrying this gratitude with you throughout the day.

Evening Reflection Meditation

Purpose: To reflect on the day, release any remaining tension, and prepare for a restful night's sleep.

Instructions:

- Lie down or sit comfortably, eyes closed, taking slow, deep breaths.
- Mentally scan through your day, recalling both challenges and victories.
- Release any tension or negativity by imagining it dissolving with each exhale.
- Reflect on the positive moments, no matter how small.
- Repeat: "I release the day with peace. I am grateful for the lessons and blessings it brought. "I welcome rest and renewal."
- Take a final breath and allow yourself to relax fully, preparing for deep, restorative sleep.

These resources and meditations are just the beginning—there's a whole world of wisdom waiting to be explored. Let your intuition guide you to what resonates and remember that the most powerful tool you have is your willingness to grow, evolve, and embrace the journey ahead! Happy exploring!

About The Author

Jamie O'Neill is an author, spiritual life coach, and holistic healing practitioner whose work is rooted in raw truth, resilience, and radical self-love. With a past marked by trauma, addiction, and transformation, she channels her experiences into deeply honest writing that empowers others to own their stories and reclaim their power. Jamie is the creator of the *Journey of My Soul* series, including her guided journal and oracle deck, which serve as tools for self-discovery, healing, and spiritual awakening.

Known for her blend of soulful insight, unfiltered humor, and no-nonsense compassion, Jamie is passionate about helping others break free from societal expectations and live in alignment with their truth.

When she's not writing or coaching, you'll find her sipping kava, singing karaoke, and traveling the world in search of inspiration, connection, and the next great story.

She believes your past does not define you—your *healing* does. And she's living proof that you can rise from the ashes, rewrite your story, and make your mess your message.

Connect with Jamie

To explore Jamie's spiritual coaching, holistic healing services, or to book a tarot reading, visit www.silvermoonholistic.com.
You can also find her latest blog posts and astrological insights at www.theastroalchemist.blogspot.com.
Learn more about her books, appearances and upcoming projects at www.jamieloneill.com.

www.ingramcontent.com/pod-product-compliance
Lightning Source LLC
Chambersburg PA
CBHW070911120626
46546CB00001B/223